Privacy, Data Protection and Cybersecurity in Europe

Wolf J. Schünemann • Max-Otto Baumann
Editors

Privacy, Data Protection and Cybersecurity in Europe

 Springer

Editors
Wolf J. Schünemann
Institute for Social Sciences
Hildesheim University
Hildesheim, Germany

Max-Otto Baumann
German Development Institute
Bonn, Germany

ISBN 978-3-319-53633-0   ISBN 978-3-319-53634-7   (eBook)
DOI 10.1007/978-3-319-53634-7

Library of Congress Control Number: 2017936666

Printed on acid-free paper

This Springer imprint is published by Springer Nature
The registered company is Springer International Publishing AG
The registered company address is: Gewerbestrasse 11, 6330 Cham, Switzerland

Preface

When we first discussed the idea of gathering an international group of scholars for a workshop on privacy and data protection in Europe, we had a comparative enquiry of the national traditions, practices and discourses regarding this field of growing importance in the era of digitisation in mind. Given the developments in European policymaking (the General Data Protection Regulation was entering the final stage of the regulatory process in Brussels), itself a reaction to the profound change brought by digitisation, the time was certainly right for this academic endeavour. Confirming our first guess, we quickly learned that despite the obvious practical relevance, there is indeed a large research gap on these issues that calls to be addressed. When receiving paper proposals, we also recognised that the Snowden revelations of 2013 strongly affected the political discussions on the issue as well as the scholarly work. We faced a complex ensemble of intertwined issues which included privacy, data protection and cybersecurity. For the programme of our workshop, which took place in Heidelberg in November 2015, and for this book, we decided to take up this integrated perspective and include chapters that concentrate either on one of the main fields or their mutual interferences.

The workshop would not have taken place and this book would have never reached publication without the financial and organisational support of several institutions and the help and engagement of several people. First of all, we want to express our gratitude to the Fritz Thyssen Foundation for supporting the workshop in Heidelberg with essential funding. For the preparation of the workshop and especially the publication process, we received additional funding from the Field of Focus 4: Self-Regulation and Regulation (Excellence Initiative of the German Research Association) at Heidelberg University. Once again, we enjoyed the reliable and competent assistance of Sabine Falke who deserves our personal gratitude. Besides that, our workshop included a group visit to the Center for Art and Media (ZKM) in Karlsruhe where the fantastic exhibition Global Control and Censorship constituted a perfect supplement to our workshop. Our special thanks for making this possible go to the curators Bernhard Serexhe and Lívia Nolasco-Rozsas. We also have to give credit to the John Stuart Mill Institute in Heidelberg where the idea for this project originally emerged from and which served as our partner in the organisation of the workshop. For informal support on all stages, we want to thank the members of the Netzpolitik AG (Internet Governance Group) at Heidelberg University.

For the English language proofreading, our thanks go to Zachary Hunter. The linguistic and stylistic quality of the chapters greatly benefited from his corrections. Last but definitely not least, we want to thank all student assistants who were engaged in different stages of the project. We want to express our particular gratitude to Maria Stalla for holding all threads together during the organisation and implementation of the workshop. For the second phase and especially for the final stage of the editing process, our special thanks go to Louisa Well, who has patiently managed the proofreading and copy-editing process with great competence.

Hildesheim, Germany   Wolf J. Schünemann
Bonn, Germany   Max-Otto Baumann
December 2016

Contents

Part III Europeanisation: Centre and Periphery

List of Contributors

Ana Azurmendi, Ph.D. is Professor of Media Law at the Faculty of Communication of the University of Navarra since 1991. Her main fields of interest are privacy, digital rights, public service media and copyright.

Max-Otto Baumann, Dr. is a researcher at the Deutsches Institut für Entwicklungspolitik/German Development Institute. Before that, he was a researcher at the John Stuart Mill Institute where he focused on privacy studies.

Katharina Dimmroth, M.A. is a researcher and doctoral student at the Institute of Political Science at RWTH Aachen. Her main fields of interest are US Foreign Policy, US Security Policy and German Foreign Policy.

Bernhard Gross, Ph.D. is Associate Professor at the University of the West of England. His main research interests are focused on the impact of emerging technologies on journalistic practice and on the representation of social issues in the public sphere.

Lina Jasmontaite, L.L.M. is a legal researcher at the Vrije Universiteit in Brussels. Her research interests include law, science, technology and society.

Valentina Pavel Burloiu, L.L.M. is a legal researcher and digital rights advocate focusing on privacy, Internet freedom and open culture. She is also involved with ApTI—the Association for Technology and Internet, member of EDRi—European Digital Rights.

Ariadna Ripoll Servent, Dr. is Junior Professor of Political Science and European Integration at the University of Bamberg. Her research interests include European institutions, institutional and policy change as well as EU internal security policies.

Wolf J. Schünemann, Dr. is Junior Professor of Political Science at Hildesheim University. His main fields of interest are Internet governance, political online communication, European integration and discourse studies.

Stefan Steiger, M.A. is a researcher and doctoral student at the Institute of Political Science of the University of Heidelberg. His main fields of interest are cybersecurity, Internet governance and foreign policy analysis.

Minna Tiainen, M.A. is a researcher and doctoral student at the University of Jyväskylä. Her main fields of interest are Critical Discourse Studies, media and surveillance.

Verena Weiland, M.A. is a researcher and doctoral student at Heidelberg University and Université Paris-Est. Weiland's main fields of interest are Discourse Analysis, Semantics and Critique of Language.

Introduction: Privacy, Data Protection and Cybersecurity in Europe

The Conceptual and Factual Field

Max-Otto Baumann and Wolf J. Schünemann

This book is about privacy, data protection and cybersecurity in Europe. It is not a normative book: It neither joins the chorus of alarmist voices that lament the alleged death of privacy nor warn either against the 'cyberwar' to come (Arquilla and Ronfeldt 1997; Stone 2013) or the alleged political attempts to securitise the issue (Gorr and Schünemann 2013; Hansen and Nissenbaum 2009). It also does not offer prescriptions for how to deal with the challenges of data protection and cybersecurity (Andress and Winterfeld 2011; Eckert 2014; Kubieziel 2012). Rather, the book is a contribution to the fledgling field of theoretical and comparative approaches in the study of the digital transformation and the increasing political challenges it generates. All aspects of society are affected by digitisation. Whether we look at individuals, the economy or the state, the digitisation vastly increases opportunities and risks, but it does so in uneven ways, fundamentally reshaping the societal balance of power and interests and straining the values and norms of society.

Against this backdrop, we can identify privacy and cybersecurity as political meta-phenomena that constitute major challenges of our time. Data protection and computer security have now become the objects of daily concern, of contentious political issues and of global affairs, as we have observed in a continuous row of international controversies (see for instance the Sony hack from 2014, the incidents at the German Bundestag in 2015, the safe harbour judgement of the ECJ or the incidents during the 2016 US Presidential Election campaign). Individual countries, the European Union and even the United Nations have responded to the change caused by digitisation (Neuneck 2013). One of the first regulations in the field of

M.-O. Baumann
Deutsches Institut für Entwicklungspolitik, Bonn, Germany
e-mail: max.baumann@die-gdi.de

W.J. Schünemann (✉)
Hildesheim University, Hildesheim, Germany
e-mail: wolf.schuenemann@uni-hildesheim.de

© Springer International Publishing AG 2017
W.J. Schünemann, M.-O. Baumann (eds.), *Privacy, Data Protection and Cybersecurity in Europe*, DOI 10.1007/978-3-319-53634-7_1

data protection was Germany's right of informational self-determination, created in 1982 (Busch and Jakobi 2011), that has informed similar regulations in other countries. While there is a vast amount of academic literature on privacy in general, it is almost surprising how little social science literature exists on this topic. This is particularly true for political science, which for too long has treated privacy and data protection, if at all, as almost non-political, narrowly confined policy issues. This is no longer justified, and this book is going to address this important gap.

But what do we understand by privacy, data protection and cybersecurity? How do these main concepts of this book relate to each other? Beginning with the most clearly identifiable issue, at least from a policy-making perspective: data protection refers to personal data and the rules that apply to the processing of these data. Every society is based on the exchange of personal information, and thus data protection is not so much about keeping one's data isolated, but rather the rules and options regarding the transmission and use of these data. The current regime of data protection in Europe is largely based on the notion of user consent and control, according to which individuals can decide for themselves which data they want to share with whom and for what purposes (cf. Cate and Mayer-Schönberger 2013; Schermer et al. 2014). But it also involves general rules including the principle of data parsimony, purpose specification, data quality and security safeguards. All these principles can be derived from ethical considerations and are recognised by international and customary law (Baumann 2015). Especially the latter set of principles, which imposes restrictions on the data user, is increasingly relevant in the era of digitisation as the generation, the processing and trade of/with personal data have become part and parcel of digital economies.

Data protection is closely related to privacy, which is more difficult to define. Philosophy has a long tradition of debating what privacy is (Solove 2002; Nissenbaum 1998; Rössler 2001), but in the context of digitisation, privacy protection can be understood as referring not to the decisional or spatial, but to the informational aspect of privacy. As stated above, the precedential judgement of the German Constitutional Court from 1982 is based on that dimension of privacy, and the right of informational self-determination has since become the cornerstone of privacy protection regimes. These also include in a broader sense data protection authorities, self-regulation strategies and technical rules (like "opt-in", "opt-out"). According to the principle of informational self-determination, the level of privacy is determined by the ability of individuals to decide themselves which data they share with whom and for which purposes. As such, we can treat data protection as the instrument for privacy protection, recognising of course that privacy has other dimensions beyond the transmission, storage and processing of personal data. We suggest thinking of the relationship of the two concepts in terms of a hierarchy, where the right to privacy is a fundamental right, based on ethical considerations and internationally recognised, from which data protection norms are derived and that is guaranteed by data protection regimes.

Let us turn to cybersecurity, which is related to the other two concepts. First of all, in the digitised society, cybersecurity (IT security or data security) has become in a narrow sense a fundamental precondition for the protection of personal data.

Most legal documents reflect this basic requirement and prescribe measures to protect personal data on a given system against unauthorised access. For example, the new EU data protection directive in article 29 requires the controllers and processors of data "to implement appropriate technical and organisational measures to ensure a level of security appropriate to the risk".[1] While data security can thus be seen as a precondition for data protection, cybersecurity is a much broader concept. It includes many concerns, such as infrastructure and economic security, which are not related to personal data at all. The societal and political understandings of cybersecurity even include many connotations that do not have much to do with IT and computer systems neither—a problem that is discussed at length in other works (Nissenbaum 2005). Differentiated by its core objectives—confidentiality, integrity and availability (the so-called CIA triad of cybersecurity, Singer and Friedman 2014)—data protection is closely related only to two of the three goals, namely the integrity of computer systems and the confidentiality of the data stored therein. Therefore, data protection and cybersecurity do not always go hand in hand; they can conflict with each other. The discussion about anonymity in IT usage or online communication, with the desire to communicate anonymously pitted against the interest of criminal investigators in potentially authenticating all internet users, serves as a good illustration in this regard. Generally speaking, for the security administrator of a computer system/network, the distinct authentication of all users/parties on the system/within the network is an important desideratum. However, the user of a particular service or internet communication in general might be interested in anonymity. More fundamentally, anonymous communication is an existential condition for the freedom of speech or democratic activism.

All those difficult facets of the relationship between privacy/data protection and cybersecurity take us to a traditional controversy of values or, more explicitly, into the fundamental dilemma of freedom vs. security. As not only the 2013 revelations by Edward Snowden rendered visible, much that has endangered the privacy and thus civil freedoms of people around the world has been done and justified for the sake of advancing (cyber-)security. In the next section, this introductory chapter delves a bit deeper into this fundamental relation by starting with an actor-centred conceptualisation of the field as a "ménage à trois". From there, we describe data protection as a political challenge. As to academic research in the field, we give an overview in another section. For cybersecurity, we combine the literature overview with the dissection of securitisation theory, which is the leading approach to studying cybersecurity. At the end of this chapter, we present an outline of the entire book.

---

[1]Directive (EU) 2016/680 of the European Parliament and of the Council of 27 April 2016. The OECD also spells out in its Privacy Guidelines from 1980 a security safeguards principle according to which "Personal data should be protected by reasonable security safeguards against such risks as loss or unauthorised access, destruction, use, modification or disclosure of data." (OECD 2013: 23).

1   Ménage à Trois under Stress: Data Protection in the Digital Age

Traditionally, the right to privacy has been seen as a liberal defensive law meant to protect individual freedom against the control of society. Warren and Brandeis, widely recognised as the inventors of the right to privacy, did not have the state in mind when they formulated the right "to be let alone" (1890). Today, the right to privacy as a fundamental right and a key element of international human rights is primarily meant to protect individuals against intrusive surveillance from the state. It is enshrined in core documents of international law such as the Universal Declaration of Human Rights (Art. 12) and the European Convention on Human Rights (Art. 8). However, the more personal data become a tradable good—a development clearly accelerated by digitisation—, the more the corporate sector with an interest in economic gains also becomes an aggressor in this sense. However, these roles are not fixed. After the Snowden revelations, large internet companies defended their customers' privacy rights against state surveillance. Therefore, in this trilateral constellation, the corporate sector and the state can appear in both roles as protector and violator of citizens/customers (and this arguably also holds for private surveillance in citizen-citizen-relationships).

Thus, a modern data protection regulation must deal with an ensemble of interrelations that emerge from three ideal-typical actor categories. Visualised in Fig. 1, we describe this as a "ménage à trois". Regulation and self-regulation in the field of privacy and data protection must reflect the relationships of individual users or citizens towards public agencies of all sorts or the state. This is the classical dimension where many actual data protection rules have their origins as elements of a liberal defensive law, including Germany's right to informational self-determination from 1982, which was created in the wake of a census (Busch and Jakobi 2011; Berlinghoff 2013). Regarding this dimension, cleavages are rather obvious, as they are rooted in civic freedom and human dignity vs. security and control. This first dimension was almost forgotten in an era of unworried internet

Fig. 1 Ménage à trois

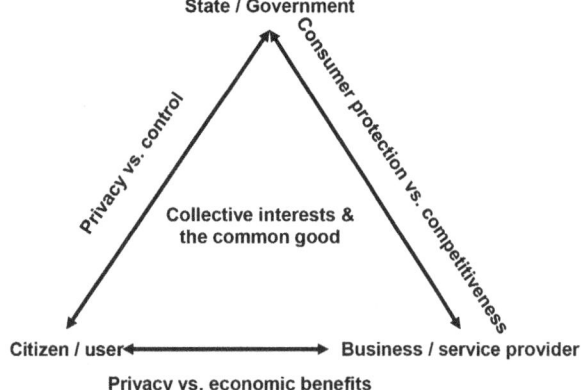

use, culminating in the rapid rise of social media with its inherent privacy problematic, but it has once again gained public attention as Snowden revelations have been published piece-by-piece, giving more and more insight into governmental mass surveillance practices in the digital age.

However, despite the increased knowledge on surveillance, agencies of the public sector are of course not the only institutional actors that process personal data. With the growing digital economy, electronically stored and transferred data have become an extremely important resource for a large field of economic activity. Huge amounts of metadata, content and personal information are gathered, processed and analysed by firms for profit on a daily basis in order to offer individualised services to users or to design more efficient systems in various sectors such as healthcare, public transportation and insurance. With these new forms of economic activity, the ménage à trois has got a completely different accentuation. As Cohen (2013), for instance, made clear, data protection, starting as a protective right in liberal terms closely related to individualism, has become much more important to be valued and secured in relation to business firms of the internet economy. Often, there are direct benefits from giving personal data to providers or apps for the individuals whose data are processed. But the chilling effects of a panoptical digital surveillance architecture (Bentham 2003 [1791]; Foucault 1981) that no longer allows for effective informational self-determination are of course also not to be underestimated. Cohen (2013) is thus right about the fact that the conditioning of our lives by services and applications based on data analysis is worrisome.

The third leg refers to the relationship between state and economy. Until the Snowden affair, the economy was seen as hostile to privacy issues, but the disclosure of enforced collaborations between business and state regarding intelligence and criminal investigations has led to a new situation. Faced with consumer distrust, some large companies have switched sides and are now holding up the privacy claims of their users to fend off state surveillance. This obviously leads us back to the meaning of data protection as a liberal protective law as the state, with its panoptical tendencies, is engaged as an actor behind the scenes, monitoring and controlling digital communication and service consumption that is supposed to be 'private' from the user's perspective.

Yet, the state also has the role of a privacy regulator in this relationship. The central cleavage is between consumer protection on the one hand and economic competitiveness on the other. Effective data protection requires that the state enact and enforce laws and regulations; even self-regulation takes place within guidelines set by the state. However, especially in the European context, the argument has been made that too restrictive data protection rules could harm the competitiveness of European businesses in relation to US internet firms, increasing the comparative advantages of the latter in this sector. Moreover, on the level of international economics, some US firms argued that data protection regulation in Europe was a new form of protectionism and an attempt to narrow the developmental gap between internet industries on both sides of the Atlantic, a criticism shared even by U.S. president Obama (Washington Post 2015).

1.1 Privacy as a Political Challenge

As briefly stated above, the current regime of data protection is mostly based on the concept of informational self-determination, by which individuals decide for themselves which data they share with whom and for what purposes. According to this view, users have the power to determine how much privacy they want in their interactions with Google, Facebook and other firms. This non-political paradigm of privacy protection was complemented by the assumption that data privacy could be left to the self-regulation of data processing economies. Firms were expected to respect consumers' privacy interests for the sake of staying in business.

However, there are important prerequisites to self-responsibility which are becoming increasingly problematic: users have to know about the storage, transfer and processing of their data in order to make informed decisions, and their decisions must be free from external force. But many internet services, especially social networks, profit from very powerful network effects, which give them monopolistic positions. Users tend to accept the terms in order to be part of the vast community that is available from the largest network. Not being part of one particular network (e.g. Facebook) might equal being isolated from a social group and cut off from its informational streams. In general, avoiding services for the sake of privacy becomes increasingly difficult in societies where social and technical infrastructures are widely digitised. The premise of individual control is especially problematic in social groups that require special protection, e.g. children, old or disabled persons. The reliance on self-responsibility would turn out harmful for them and would stand in conflict with normative principles of any given society.

Thus, scholars have argued that with the exponential increase in data flows, the technical and economic complexity of big data processing technology and the lack of real choice, the data protection regime should no longer be based on individual consent and control, as the prerequisites for individual self-determination no longer exist (Schermer et al. 2014; Cate and Mayer-Schönberger 2013). If that assessment is correct, then data protection evolves from a matter of personal self-determination to an issue of general rules on the processing of data. And with that, it becomes a topic for a genuinely political analysis. The practice of data processing and the privacy rules that govern it are an issue for political analysis, because these rules now decide on the allocation of material and immaterial values to an extent that was unimaginable when the internet was simply an instrument for selected purposes. In the 1990s, the American scholar Priscilla Regan was the first to argue that the digital transformation should not only be analysed in terms of individual rights but also in terms of societal effects. "Our thinking on privacy needs to turn outward, to its importance to social, political, and economic relationships [...] and to our common public life more generally" (Regan 1995: 242).

It has now become obvious that the practice of privacy—to what extent and in what contexts it is granted or compromised—has real "redistributive effects" (Bennett and Raab 2006: 38). In a report commissioned by the White House, the authors note that the level of privacy increasingly defines "chances, opportunities, prizes" in life (Podesta 2014)—and although this statement is about individuals, something similar could be said about firms and the state and their respective interests. Data processing affects the distribution of costs, benefits, security and risks between individuals, companies and the state. It is thus not just a technical issue of judicial concern but essentially a political issue, as the policy field of data protection fulfils the very definition of the political function according to the famous system theorist of politics David Easton: "the authoritative allocation of values" (Easton 1965), both material and immaterial.

Data protection as an individual goal competes with collective interests of society like public order, security, public health, public moral, the privacy and freedom of others, freedom of information—all these are internationally recognised principles that justify the limitation of privacy. Taking the analysis from the individual to the social level, Bennett and Raab (2006: 24) argue that privacy is also related to the amount of "equity, trust, and risk" in a society. From this observation, we can hypothesise that societies with a greater emphasis on equity and trust and a greater aversion to risk might prefer stricter privacy laws, but causality might also run in the other direction. Privacy should therefore not only be seen as a liberal norm, but as a political issue playing host to conservative and social-democratic perspectives that emphasise different values.

The abovementioned observations are hardly innovative or surprising. We can almost state them as a matter of fact. It is all the more surprising that the diagnosis of Bennett and Raab, now a decade old, still appears to be true today. "There is no tradition of studying information privacy within the academic discipline of political science, and thus no identifiable tradition or cumulative literature upon which to draw" (Bennett and Raab 2006: xix). We agree with them that we "need to pay closer attention to the regulation of personal information as a major 'currency' of both the contemporary capitalist organization and of the modern state" (Bennett and Raab 2006: xix). This new field of study requires the development of new theories—in particular from political science, but with the help and in a fruitful exchange with neighbouring disciplines.

1.2 Comparative Analysis of Data Protection

Every society can be expected to have found a different balance to the various interests represented in the ménage à trois (see above). This might have to do with the degree of digitisation in a society, path dependencies of laws that are already in place, economic cultures, citizen-state relationships and historical identities. Most of these factors are not so much given but constructed in discourses. Widening the scope of the analysis to Europe—a geographic area with sufficient cultural homogeneity, yet notable differences in privacy attitudes and levels of privacy protection (Eurobarometer 2011)—offers an opportunity for comparative analysis. Bennett and Raab correctly observed that "privacy protection is an excellent issue for comparative studies of how the same problems are resolved in different countries, and what this says about their institutional and cultural capacities to shape techno-logical change" (Bennett and Raab 2006: xxi). At the same time, it is surprising how little analysis has been conducted in this field so far (see as notable exceptions, Capurro 2005; Greenleaf 2013; Rule and Greenleaf 2008; Westin 1970). We know so little about this field that currently there can only be wild guesses of how the European privacy legislation will be received in various European countries or what the chances and pitfalls of a global regulation would be.

We do not offer an elaborate framework for a comparative study of privacy in this book. The research assembled in this book provides some insights into open questions and indicates where further research is warranted. In the preview of the literature, we point out some issues for a comparative analysis of privacy and cybersecurity that arise from the contributions to this book.

2 Cybersecurity and the Tempting Story of Securitisation

Researchers of cybersecurity entered the scene in the late 1990s, first of all in the context of the US American security sector, with alarmist warnings against a global cyberwar to come (Arquilla and Ronfeldt 1997). This alarmism has left deep traces in parts of the academic discourse and—more clearly—in many publications oriented towards a broader public (Gaycken 2012) and therewith public discourse itself. On the other hand, the more popular scientific notions of cyberwar, cyberterrorism, etc. have provoked more serious (cyber-)security scholars to reveal the metaphors as more or less meaningless exaggerations (Rid 2012) or to study the structural effects language can produce in its performative quality as speech acts in the sense of securitisation theory (Balzacq 2011; Buzan et al. 1998). Securitisation has become the probably most frequently applied theoretical approach in cyberse-curity studies (Dunn Cavelty 2013; Gorr and Schünemann 2013; Guitton 2013; Hansen and Nissenbaum 2009). The shared story that unfolds from these works is tempting and of course quite plausible: governmental actors and other stakeholders in the security subsystem, driven by interest or conviction, construct phenomena of the cyber world, maybe cyberspace itself, as a security problem by discursive action. If this is accepted and shared by the audience, extraordinary political measures might be legitimated, including increased surveillance and control. As cybersecurity is a very broad concept (see above) which includes security concerns that are not connected to the confidentiality, integrity and availability of computer systems, it comes as no surprise that the concept tends to interfere with or contradict core IT security goals (Nissenbaum 2005).

Comparative studies in the field of cybersecurity have concentrated either on the comparison of motives, institutions and competences of nation states and interna-tional organisations (Billo and Chang 2004; Lewis and Neuneck 2013) or on incidents that have been relevant to cybersecurity (Lewis and CSIS 2015; Valeriano and Maness 2014). The first strand is rather technical and descriptive in its basic design. What is more, hidden programs that might be even more relevant, e.g. for assessing the offensive or defensive potential of a state or organisation, can per definition not be reflected in the data set and discussion. A similar problem of opacity exists with regard to the challenge of attribution, which for cyberattacks mostly cannot be done with sufficient certainty as to warrant sanctions (Rid and Buchanan 2015). This challenge also affects the second strand of research on cybersecurity incidents, and even more so, as agency would be one indicator to differentiate attacks from each other. What projects (or better: archives) of this sort often lack is a clear systematic methodology which would allow for more comparative operations than simply the bringing of anecdotal evidence into a chronological order. One way to deal with that challenge is to put greater emphasis on the specificity of cybersecurity discourses in different countries. From there, institutional developments and open and hidden activities might be much more understandable. As the issue of cybersecurity has been rather underrepresented in the broader public discourse, it is important to note that just as for privacy/data protection, the recent Snowden revelations (2013) have brought the issue of cybersecurity to the fore. This is why we included in this volume a number of contributions that deal with cybersecurity discourses in one or more countries and that allow for important comparative insights.

3 Outline of the Book

The book's first section presents chapters that deal with some fundamental issues regarding the regulation of privacy and data protection. Both contributions have a strong country focus, namely Spain and the United Kingdom.

The contribution from Ana Azurmendi analyses how one of the European Union's most notable legal innovations of the internet era, the legal principle of the "right to be forgotten", emerged from interactions with the Spanish judiciary. The Spanish National High Court triggered a preliminary procedure at the European Court of Justice to clarify an ambiguity in the right of informational self-determination, a right that was already well established in the Spanish legal system. Through its decision, the European Court of Justice established what became known as the "right to be forgotten". Azurmendi reconstructs the arguments made by the courts and by the defendant, the company Google. In her analysis it becomes clear that at the heart of the matter lies a conflict between citizen and business interests, which encompasses ramifications for the common good as well. The new right to be forgotten arguably marks a decisive victory for individual rights. The European Court of Justice stated that it "override[s], as a rule, not only the economic interest of the operator of the search engine but also the interest of the general public in having access to that information". Although Azurmendi does not address this aspect, it is worth pointing out that strong criticism was levelled against this new legal principle from abroad, with an editorial from the New York Times lambasting it as a threat to the freedom of information (New York

Times, 4th February 2015). This suggests that other cultures might prefer a very different balance of interests than the one created in the European Union.

Bernhard Gross takes the review of data protection and privacy in Europe to the field of social media journalism in the UK. In contrast to the Spanish system, the regime of privacy and data protection in the UK rests on basic human rights norms, case law and self-regulation. Focusing on self-regulation, Gross adopts an exploratory approach to disentangle the interests involved in and the logic of privacy protection in the UK. In two case studies, he identifies the tensions between a journalist's practical interest in obtaining direct and sometimes sensational information from social media and the privacy claims of the affected individuals. The analysis conveys a picture of privacy as vulnerable in the face of a highly fragmented and perennially outdated, yet flexibly adjusting system of self-regulation. According to Gross, this system is retained due to a concern shared equally by the state and by journalists, namely that a more legally robust privacy law would limit the freedom of information.

In the second part of the book, we shift our view to different national cybersecurity discourses. These are studied in analyses of the debates on the Snowden revelations in Finland, France, Germany and the United Kingdom.

Among the discourse analytical studies of cybersecurity debates, the one by Verena Weiland on the French debate is the most explicit on the methods used. Starting from the question of what makes the Snowden revelations an event in public discourse, she collected data from the French media debate queried by a set of pre-selected terms. Throughout her analysis, Weiland illustrates a sequence of corpus analytical tools. Her findings develop from simple facts and co-occurrences from the discourse in question to deeper insights about the patterns of the French reactions to the mass surveillance revelations. Weiland's analysis shows that French reactions to the Snowden revelations were directed towards the regulatory issue of data protection more than towards the more arcane (cyber)security issue. Moreover, she identifies an orientation towards the German debate, where data protection traditionally is a more salient issue than in its western neighbour society.

Tiainen's study on cybersecurity applies a different discourse analytical approach; she combines Critical Discourse Studies with Surveillance Studies. Similar to the other chapters in this part of the book, she focusses on state-citizen relations that are dealt with in public debates on unwanted surveillance and especially the solutions to problems presented by media actors. Coming with an analytical focus on discursive struggles in general, the article particularly aims at patterns or elements of contestation of surveillance in the Finnish newspaper *Helsingin Sanomat*. The main interpretive schemes that Tiainen identifies are what she calls "next step" and "direct" solutions. Tiainen draws the conclusion that all in all, not many solutions are presented, which is partly due to surveillance being an issue beyond daily politics and partly due to the rather high level of technical knowledge necessary for the understanding and explanation of signal intelligence so that such articles are not very likely to appear in a daily newspaper.

Stefan Steiger sheds light on the "unshaken role of GCHQ" in the British cybersecurity discourse. As in the other discourse analytical chapters in this part of the book, he focusses on the governmental surveillance practices and the liberal defensive contestation that should have been triggered by the Snowden revelations. He analyses relevant governmental and parliamentary documents complemented by texts from the UK Government Communications Headquarters (GCHQ) that were published after the Snowden revelations. Based on a role theoretical perspective, Steiger examines the reasons for the relatively little critique of surveillance practices and the lack of any consequences for the regulation of intelligence services. He identifies the historical self as well as the special functional scope of GCHQ as being most influential. For the author, both factors helped to uphold a positive perception of the British intelligence services even after 2013.

Katharina Dimmroth and Wolf Schünemann combine the two main issues of this book, privacy/data protection and cybersecurity, in their study on post-Snowden discourses in German parliament and government. By analysing and reconstructing problem definitions and solutions that are proposed and discussed by the different sets of speakers they try to disentangle the two phenomena or issues in how they are discursively constructed. The authors find that discursive patterns in both fields are influenced by an underlying meta-narrative of cyberspace as a dangerous place (so-called cyber anxiety). Also, they identify different discursive patterns on how the fundamental values of privacy and (cyber-)security are hierarchically ordered.

In the last part of the book, two chapters examine processes of Europeanisation on the European Union level as well as within different member states. While chapter "Protecting or Processing?" focusses on data protection regulation, it is the European cybersecurity directive (called NIS Directive) that stands central in the case studies of chapter "Lithuania and Romania to Introduce Cybersecurity Laws".

Ariadna Ripoll Servent does not focus on a specific country but rather the European level. We found it worthwhile to integrate the supranational European perspective in the book. In the end, privacy and data protection call for European (if not global) solutions. Ripoll Servent analyses the negotiation process that led to the EU's new data protection regime, which was finally agreed on in 2016. In particular, she addresses the tension between the two "logics", or roots, of data protection in the EU and to what extent they were harmonised: data protection in the single market (resulting in the new "Regulation") and in the field of security (resulting in the lesser known "Directive"). Ripoll Servent finds that in the end there was no real compromise, with the Directive lagging behind the Regulation in terms of data protection. But perhaps more importantly than that, the article reveals a complex net of political interests that surrounds the regulation of privacy protection. The European Parliament pushed for high data protection levels, emphasising individual rights, while governments tended to prioritise economic liberty and security. However, parliamentarians were by no means unified. Different parties held widely different opinions on how to balance data protection and privacy rights with economic liberty and public security. Centre-right parties gravitated toward the government position, while left-leaning parties were more consumer-friendly.

Finally, Lina Jasmontaite and Valentina Pavel Burloiu present a comparative study of the design and the implementation of cybersecurity laws in Lithuania and Romania. As members of the European Union, both countries are affected by the regulatory efforts at the EU level, namely the Network and Information Security Directive (NIS Directive). As there is a controversial debate on the compatibility of some provisions derived from the NIS directive with international human rights standards, the authors reflect on the two cases with a human rights approach which they combine with the concept of "good regulation" by Baldwin and Cave. In conclusion, they present different inconsistencies in how the directive is implemented in the two Eastern European countries as well as important insights on the different public reactions to cybersecurity regulation there.

References

Andress, J., & Winterfeld, S. (2011). *Cyber warfare techniques. Tactics and tools for security practitioners*. Amsterdam, Heidelberg [u.a.], Waltham, MA: Elsevier Syngress.

Arquilla, J., & Ronfeldt, D. (1997). Cyberwar is coming! In J. Arquilla & D. Ronfeldt (Eds.), *In Athena's camp. Preparing for conflict in the information age* (pp. 23–60). Santa Monica, CA: Rand.

Balzacq, T. (2011). A theory of securitization. Origins, core assumptions, and variants. In T. Balzacq (Ed.), *PRIO new security studies. Securitization theory. How security problems emerge and dissolve* (1st ed., pp. 1–30). London [u.a.]: Routledge.

Baumann, M.-O. (2015). *Privatsphäre als neues digitales Menschenrecht? Ethische Prinzipien und aktuelle Diskussionen*. Hamburg: DIVSI Diskussionsbeiträge.

Bennett, C. J., & Raab, C. (2006). *The governance of privacy. Policy instruments in global perspective*. Cambridge: MIT Press.

Bentham, J. (2003 [1791]). *Panopticon: or, the inspection-house. Containing the idea of a new principle of construction applicable to any sort of establishment, in which persons of any Description are to be kept under Inspection. and in particular to penitentiary-houses, prisons, Houses of Industry, Work-Houses, Poor-Houses, Manufactories, Mad-Houses, Hospitals, and Schools. With a plan of Management adapted to the Principle. In a series of letters, written in the Year 1787, From Crecheff in White Russia, to a Friend in England*. Dublin: Eighteenth Century Collections Online. http://find.galegroup.com/ecco/infomark.do?&source=gale&prodId=ECCO&userGroupName=heidel&tabID=T001&docId=CW125793319&type=multipage&contentSet=ECCOArticles&version=1.0&docLevel=FASCIMILE

Berlinghoff, M. (2013). "Totalerfassung" im "Computerstaat"—Computer und Privatheit in den 1970er und 1980er Jahren. In U. Ackermann (Ed.), *Im Sog des Internets. Öffentlichkeit und Privatheit im digitalen Zeitalter* (pp. 93–110). Frankfurt am Main: Humanities Online.

Billo, C. G., & Chang, W. (2004). *Cyber warfare. An analysis of the means and motivations of selected nation states*. Dartmouth.

Busch, A., & Jakobi, T. (2011). Die Erfindung eines neuen Grundrechts: Zu Konzept und Auswirkungen der "informationellen Selbstbestimmung". In C. Hönnige, S. Kneip, & A. Lorenz (Eds.), *Verfassungswandel im Mehrebenensystem* (pp. 297–320). Wiesbaden: VS Verlag für Sozialwissenschaften.

Buzan, B., Waever, O., & de Wilde, J. (1998). *Security: A new framework for analysis*. Boulder, CO: Lynne Rienner.

Capurro, R. (2005). Privacy. An intercultural perspective. *Ethics and Information Technology, 7*, 37–47.

Cate, F. H., & Mayer-Schönberger, V. (2013). Tomorrow's privacy. Notice and consent in a world of Big Data. *International Data Privacy Law, 3*(2), 67–73.

Cohen, J. E. (2013). What privacy is for. *Harvard Law Review, 126*, 1904–1933.

Dunn Cavelty, M. (2013). Der Cyber-Krieg, der (so) nicht kommt: Erzählte Katastrophen als (Nicht)Wissenspraxis. In L. Hempel & M. Bartels (Eds.), *Sozialtheorie. Aufbruch ins Unversicherbare. Zum Katastrophendiskurs der Gegenwart* (2nd ed., pp. 209–233). Bielefeld: Transcript.

Easton, D. (1965). *A systems analysis of political life.* New York: Wiley.

Eckert, C. (2014). *IT-Sicherheit: Konzepte, Verfahren, Protokolle, De Gruyter Studium* (9th ed.). Oldenbourg: de Gruyter.

Eurobarometer. (2011). Attitudes on data protection and electronic identity in the European Union. *Special Eurobarometer* 359: Brussels: European Commission.

Foucault, M. (1981). *Überwachen und Strafen: Die Geburt des Gefängnisses, Suhrkamp-Taschenbuch Wissenschaft* (Vol. 184, 4th ed.). Frankfurt am Main: Suhrkamp.

Gaycken, S. (2012). *Cyberwar. Das Wettrüsten hat längst begonnen. Vom digitalen Angriff zum realen Ausnahmezustand, Goldmann* (Vol. 15710). München: Goldmann.

Gorr, D., & Schünemann, W. J. (2013). Creating a secure cyberspace: Securitization in Internet governance discourses and dispositives in Germany and Russia. *International Review of Information Ethics, 20*(12), 37–51. http://www.i-r-i-e.net/inhalt/020/IRIE-Gorr-Schuenemann.pdf.

Greenleaf, G. (2013). Data protection in a globalised network. In I. Brown (Ed.), *Research handbook on governance of the Internet* (pp. 221–259). Cheltenham: Edward Elgar.

Guitton, C. (2013). Cyber insecurity as a national threat: Overreaction from Germany, France and the UK? *European Security, 20*(1), 21–35.

Hansen, L., & Nissenbaum, H. (2009). Digital disaster, cyber security, and the copenhagen school. *International Studies Quarterly, 53*(4), 1155–1175. doi:10.1111/j.1468-2478.2009.00572.x.

Kubieziel, J. (2012). Anonym im Netz: Wie Sie sich und Ihre Daten schützen (3rd). user space. München: Open Source Press.

Lewis, J. A., & CSIS. (2015). *Significant Cyber Incidents Since 2006.* Washington, DC. http://csis.org/files/publication/150605_Significant_Cyber_Events_List.pdf

Lewis, J. A., & Neuneck, G. (Eds.). (2013). UNIDIR: Vol. 3. *The Cyber Index: International Security Trends and Realities.* http://www.unidir.org/files/publications/pdfs/cyber-index-2013-en-463.pdf

Neuneck, G. (2013). Assessment of international and regional activities. In J. A. Lewis & G. Neuneck (Eds.), UNIDIR: Vol. 3. *The Cyber Index. International Security Trends and Realities* (pp. 91–140).

New York Times Editorial Board. (2015, 4 February). Europe's Expanding "Right to be Forgotten" (downloaded from http://www.nytimes.com/2015/02/04/opinion/europes-expanding-right-to-be-forgotten.html?_r=2).

Nissenbaum, H. (1998). Protecting privacy in an information age: The problem of privacy in public. *Law and Philosophy, 17*(5/6), 559–596.

Nissenbaum, H. (2005). Where computer security meets national security. *Ethics and Information Technology, 7*(2), 61–73. doi:10.1007/s10676-005-4582-3.

OECD. (2013). Exploring data-driven innovation as a new source of growth: Mapping the policy issues raised by "big data". *OECD Digital Economy Papers*, No. 222. OECD Publishing, http://dx.doi.org/10.1787/5k47zw3fcp43-en.

Podesta, J. (2014). *Big data: Seizing opportunities, preserving values.* Washington, DC: Executive Office of the President.

Regan, P. M. (1995). *Legislating privacy. Technology, social values, and public policy.* Chapel Hill & London: The University of North Carolina Press.

Rid, T. (2012). Cyber war will not take place. *Journal of Strategic Studies, 35*(1), 5–32. doi:10.1080/01402390.2011.608939.

Rid, T., & Buchanan, B. (2015). Attributing cyber attacks. *Journal of Strategic Studies, 38*(1–2), 4–37.

Rössler, B. (2001). *Der Wert des Privaten*. Frankfurt am Main: Suhrkamp.

Rule, J. B., & Greenleaf, G. W. (Eds.). (2008). *Global privacy protection: The first generation*. Cheltenham: Edward Elgar.

Schermer, B. W., Custers, B., & van der Hof, S. (2014). The crisis of consent: How stronger legal protection may lead to weaker consent in data protection. *Ethics and Information Technology, 2*, 171–182.

Singer, P. W., & Friedman, A. (2014). *Cybersecurity and cyberwar: What everyone needs to know*. Oxford: Oxford University Press. (What everyone needs to know).

Solove, D. J. (2002). Conceptualizing privacy. *California Law Review, 90*(4), 1087–1155.

Stone, J. (2013). Cyber war will take place! *Journal of Strategic Studies, 36*(1), 101–108. doi:10.1080/01402390.2012.730485.

Valeriano, B., & Maness, R. C. (2014). The dynamics of cyber conflict between rival antagonists, 2001-11. *Journal of Peace Research, 51*(3), 347–360. doi:10.1177/0022343313518940.

Washington Post. (2015, 17 Feb). Obama says that Europeans are using privacy rules to protect their firms against U.S. competition. Is he right? Accessed Dec 6, 2016 from https://www.washingtonpost.com/news/monkey-cage/wp/2015/02/17/obama-says-that-europeans-are-using-privacy-rules-to-protect-their-firms-against-u-s-competition-is-he-right/?utm_term=.11da12667dec

Westin, A. F. (1970). *Privacy and freedom*. London: Bodley Head.

Part I
Fundamental Issues of Privacy and Data Protection

Spain: The Right to Be Forgotten

The Right to Privacy and the Initiative Facing the New Challenges of the Information Society

Ana Azurmendi

1 Introduction

This article aims to show the current situation surrounding the right to privacy in the Spanish legal system. First of all, we look at the regulations governing the right to privacy and at the characteristics of the Spanish protection of privacy. In the second part of the chapter, we consider the current regulations on personal data protection as the grounds for new ways of protecting privacy. Finally, the chapter shows how two new rights have emerged from the legal discourse on privacy and, overall, from the regulation of the protection of personal data: informational self-determination and the right to be forgotten. This study focuses on the latter, due to the prominent role of Spanish judges in shaping the incipient right to be forgotten via interaction with the European Court of Justice in 2014.

2 Right to Privacy

2.1 The Precedents of the Spanish Right to Privacy

One of the first precedents of the right to privacy in Spain can be found in a Supreme Court decision from 6 December 1912. After a romantic relationship between a priest and a teenager was discussed in the press, the doctrine on reparations for moral damage was applied in Spain for the first time. This decision was followed by other decisions by the state and regional courts [many authors have studied the Supreme Court's decision and its influence; among them, Pérez Fuertes (2004) and,

A. Azurmendi (✉)
University of Navarra, Pamplona, Spain
e-mail: aazur@unav.es

© Springer International Publishing AG 2017
W.J. Schünemann, M.-O. Baumann (eds.), *Privacy, Data Protection and Cybersecurity in Europe*, DOI 10.1007/978-3-319-53634-7_2

previously, De la Valgoma (1983), Díez Picazo (1979), and Herrero Tejedor (1990)]. Their arguments show the remarkable influence of American and French jurisprudence, particularly in the application of the civil law principle "neminem laedere"—unfair damage cannot be caused to anybody without creating a responsibility to repairing the evil—as the starting point for building the right to privacy. American and French judges have extended the application of this principle to many acts concerning moral damage, which are different from acts against reputation.

2.2 Characteristics of Privacy Protection in Spanish Law

The protection of privacy in Spain has certain particularities. A noteworthy characteristic is the clear difference between the right to privacy and the right to one's own image. In Spain, privacy and image are regulated as if these were two substantive rights, linked to one another but different in their aims. Taking this difference into account, the right to privacy has the purpose of keeping a personal space free from the outsiders' gaze; meanwhile, the right to one's own image tries to guarantee for each person the exclusive use of his or her image. The second characteristic of the Spanish system related to privacy is the exhaustive legal regulation of the subject, based on three kinds of protection: constitutional, criminal and civil protection. These are regulated by the Constitution of 1978, art. 18 and 20, and by the Criminal Code of 1995, art. 197, respectively; and by the Civil Protection Law on the Rights of Reputation, Privacy and the Right to One's Own Image, n. 1/1982, May 5th. This broad range of laws on privacy is due to the consistent development of the "gossip" press, which is called "Prensa del Corazón" or "Periodismo Rosa" in Spanish. This began during the 1960s with magazines like ¡Hola!, a magazine that, even today, is leading in its genre with editions in other countries and languages, such as the American and British Hello!. Tabloid journalism was expanded in the late 1980s when commercial television introduced programs of similar content. Precisely this abundance of magazines and TV programs focussed on celebrities of film, television, fashion and royalty and their personal and family lives has caused a high number of cases in tribunals. In consequence, a high priority was given to the privacy rights of celebrities. The very intensity of the law's attention towards celebrities had neglected the privacy of ordinary citizens. However, the circumstances changed with the arrival of two technological innovations: databases and the internet.

2.2.1 The Protection of Personal Data

In the 1970s and 1980s, the protection of privacy, both in Spain and in other European countries, had adopted the point of view of the celebrities, and, as a main factor of danger, the media. Therefore, the principle representing this perspective is that the sphere of privacy shouldn't be violated by paparazzi, cameras or journalists. The step that followed came from a simple technological change: the transformation of big computers to manageable devices in offices, public and private institutions, hospitals, banks, university departments, stores, etc. One consequence of the usual work with these new kinds of computers in a variety of businesses, public administrative offices, banks, etc. has been the feasibility of processing personal data. The alert about the risks for privacy came from the moment in which it was easy to indiscriminately register and transfer the data of millions of citizens. This was the time of the first European Convention for the Protection of Personal Data (1981), and of the European Directive for the Protection of Personal Data (1995), and the time of the first national laws on the subject. In Spain, the first law on personal data was enacted in 1992, and it was replaced by the Law 15/1999 'de Protección de Datos personales' (Data Protection Act).

2.2.2 The Protection on the Internet

The protection on the internet, specifically when facing search engines, is the key to understanding the frontline of today's battle for privacy. From the digitisation of newspapers and the development of blogs and social networks, a strong need arose for methods of protecting privacy that were more adequate for the era of the internet. In the end, our society needs efficient regulation in order to avoid the uncontrollable dissemination of infringements against privacy; regulation that must react quickly and proportionate to the issue of offenses against privacy. Cases like *Mario Costeja v Google (2014)* or *Els Alfacs v Google (2010)* render the inefficiency of existing rules visible and voice the demand for new rights such as the right to be forgotten.

3 Data Protection and the Right of Informational Self-Determination: The Roots of the Right to Be Forgotten

3.1 Data Protection: Law 15/1999 'de Protección de Datos personales'(Data Protection Act)

In the same way that the success of Warren and Brandeis' concept of the 'right to privacy' was due to the new risks resulting from photographic technology, especially when applied by the media, the interaction of digital communication in the 1990s brought a new kind of threat to private life and, consequently, generated a new kind of right: the right to personal data protection. The main question at the time was not only privacy—which was sometimes in danger—but the real risk of manipulation in that some organization—the state, police, companies, banks, political parties, different public departments involving health, labour, etc.—could affect individuals by creating exhaustive and detailed profiles (with aspects related to a variety of interests of the institutions and businesses above). Reacting to this threat, the European Union enacted three important directives, all of which are focused on different aspects of personal data protection:

1. Directive 95/46/EC (on Personal Data) 'on the protection of individuals with regard to the processing of personal data and the free movement of such data';
2. Directive 2002/58/EC (on Privacy and Electronic Communications) 'concerning the processing of personal data and the protection of privacy in the electronic communications sector';
3. Directive 2006/24/EC (on the Retention of Data) 'on the retention of data generated or processed in connection with the provision of publicly available electronic communications services or of public communications networks'.

Following these European normative directions, Spanish regulators enacted Law 15/1999, 'de Protección de Datos Personales' (Data Protection Act). Its main purpose is "the protection of people's freedom and fundamental rights, especially their right to reputation and the right to privacy" [Article 1]. Five significant elements can be pointed out in this Data Protection Act, 1999:

1. the data protection principles [Article 4 to 12];
2. the citizen rights [Article 13 to 19], which include the right to access to personal data irrespective to location; the right to know about the existence of personal data; the right to correct data; and the right to delete data;
3. the regulation of any kind of files [Article 20 to 33];
4. the creation of the Data Protection Agency (Agencia de Protección de Datos) [Article 35 to 42];
5. infractions and sanctions [Article 43 to 49].

The Data Protection Act, 1999, intends to balance the right to reputation and privacy on the one hand, and the requirements of the state and public authorities such as governments, police, social security, the treasury of income tax departments, etc. as well as companies, on the other. It tries to guarantee fundamental rights when there is some 'necessary use' or 'interested use'. There are three principles which help in this balance:

1. the principle of quality of data: this means not only that the personal data included must be true, but also that this data can only be held for a temporary period;
2. the right to information when the data is requested by people;
3. the principle of assumed consent given to anyone who requests access to the data.

3.2   A New Constitutional Right to Informational Self-Determination

The Constitutional Court goes beyond Law 15/1999 'de Protección de Datos personales'. Following its own arguments in three resolutions dealing with data protection, the Constitutional Court has recognised a right related to privacy and the protection of personal data but, at the same time, much more focused on personal identity. The first case was the denial of information from the regional institution 'Gobierno Civil', which at that time was a representative of the central government to a citizen who was asking about personal data that was supposedly held by the 'Gobierno Civil' [STC 254/1993]. In the second case, a bank denied an employee's request to delete his medical record from the bank's database [STC 202/1999]. The third case was the constitutional procedure against articles of the Law 15/1999, 'de Protección de Datos personales' (Data Protection Act) [STC 292/2000]. The Constitutional Court states that the protection of personal data:

> ...is an answer to one new threat against human dignity and personal rights (...); and also it is, by itself, a new right or a new fundamental freedom [STC 292/2000, Fundamento jurídico 4].

This right is different from the "right to privacy", art. 18.1 CE, with which it shares the aim of an efficient protection to privacy [STC 292/2000, Fundamento jurídico 6]. The peculiarity of the right of protection of personal data lies in its different function, which is the guarantee to any individual to be in control of this data, and at a lower level, the defence of privacy [cf. STC 292/2000, Fundamento jurídico 6]. The Constitutional Court states precisely on the subject of the right of data protection:

> The object of the fundamental right of personal data protection is not only the privacy—the individual intimate data—but any kind of personal data, even if it is not intimate, when the knowledge or the use of this data by a third party can diminish the rights of a particular person. It doesn't matter if the rights concerned are or are not fundamental, because the object (of the right of personal data protection) is not only the individual intimacy—for that purpose there is the protection of art. 18.1 CE—but the personal data. Therefore, this right also has to do with the personal data which is public and accessible to anyone. But even here, the right of the protection of personal data must be efficient [STC 292/2000, Fundamento jurídico 6].

As a consequence, the protection of personal data goes beyond the right to privacy:

> ...the data protected (by the right of protection of personal data) is all that which identifies or allows the identification of one person; it can be ideological data, sexual, religious, economic data or any type; (the collection of this data and its manipulation) in particular circumstances can constitute a threat to individuals (cf. STC 292/2000, Fundamento jurídico 6).

In respect to the protection of personal data.

> ...the prerogative to dispose of, and to control personal data means that every person has the faculty to decide which parts of their data can be transferred to a third party; it doesn't matter if this third party is the state or an individual; or which personal data can be collected

by this third party. At the same time, this right allows a person to know who has access to their personal data and for what purpose. Therefore, they can oppose this possession or use (STC 292/2000, Fundamento jurídico 6).

It is precisely in this point that the right of informational self-determination connects with the right to be forgotten, a right that has been recognised only recently. Both rights can be defined as versions of the right to privacy adjusted to the information society.

4   The Right to Be Forgotten: An Aspect of the Right to Informational Self-Determination

4.1   The Spanish Initiative for the Acknowledgement of the Right to Be Forgotten

One of the first consequences of the right of informational self-determination is more effective protection against the possible threat to personal freedom posed by the power of the immense amount of collected data. It is a power which mainly lies in its capacity to predict the behaviour of millions of persons. This is made possible through the knowledge of people's interests, their personal communications, their exchanges of opinions, their favourite sites, their professional acts, their online shopping, their pictures, etc. all of which has been gathered over the past years. The power is also strengthened by the generation of digital identities which accompany citizens throughout their lives. These digital identities are built and traced by different institutions and companies on the internet and can interfere in decisions taken by others in relation to a particular person. Even one's own decision-making process can be affected, as long as the information, the offers or the advertisements that a person receives, are determined by their specific digital identity. This is the scope of vulnerabilities that need to be protected by the new versions of the right to privacy (Tene 2011).

The problem was raised in the Spanish National High Court's preliminary question towards the European Court of Justice in the case of Mario Costeja (2014), which has another precedent in Spain: the Els Alfacs case (2010). Mario Costeja had suffered damage over the years as the result of an advertisement placed in the *La Vanguardia* newspaper in 1998 for a foreclosure sale related to debts he owed to the social security administration. When the newspaper was digitalised, Google searches for the name 'Mario Costeja' revealed personal data and financial information that had become outdated. This greatly affected his professional life. At first, Costeja filed a petition before the Spanish Data Protection Agency (SDPA), requesting for the newspaper to remove the information, but his petition was not successful. The SDPA stated that the advertisement published in the *La Vanguardia* newspaper was legal and that its removal would infringe upon freedom of expression. Nevertheless, the SDPA sent a request directed to Google Spain and Google

Inc., calling upon these companies to stop indexing the aforementioned content. Google filed an appeal against the agency's decision (and other similar decisions) before the National High Court. It was this judicial authority that ultimately referred this question for a preliminary ruling to the European Court of Justice.

The Els Alfacs case concerned a company owning a campground that had been the site of a horrific tragedy in 1978 in which a truck carrying propylene exploded, killing over 200 people. In 2010 the company filed a lawsuit against Google Spain for ignoring an earlier petition requesting that the search engine stop placing news about the accident at the top of searches of the campground's name. The complainants demanded both the right to be forgotten and the company's rights to honour, privacy and self-image. The company wanted Google to filter the search results and differentiate between those who were looking for information on the tragedy and those who merely sought information about the campground, since the way Google presented the search results at that time resulted in serious damage to the company.

In both cases, the personal information involved had been disseminated in proportion to its relevance when it was initially published, but the fact that this information was still widely available to a large audience 10–15 years after the original incidents did not appear to be logical if it caused substantial moral and economic damages and the circumstances that led to its publication no longer existed.

4.2   The European Court of Justice's Sentence in the Spanish Case of Mario Costeja v. Google, May 13th, 2014

Many authors have provided exhaustive commentaries on the decision of the European Court of Justice regarding the preliminary questions raised by the Spanish National High Court on the Mario Costeja v Google case (Andrés Boix Palop 2015; Nieves Busán García 2014; Lorenzo Cotino Hueso 2015; Artemi Rallo 2014; Gregory Voss 2014). For this reason reference will only be given to arguments that are directly linked to the recognition of the right to be forgotten. The Spanish National High Court raised four doubts about the interpretation of the directive concerning Data Protection 95/46, in 2012, through three preliminary questions raised to the European Court of Justice:

1. Whether the indexation of research engines should be considered "data processing" (Preliminary question 1, part 1);
2. Whether Google.es can be considered a company headquartered in Spain or rather an affiliate of American Google (Preliminary question 1, part 2);
3. Whether the manager of a search engine must delete links to websites collected in search results (Preliminary question 2);
4. Whether an individual can request that the manager of a search engine delete both data and information if this data and information can damage them or for

the simpler reason that this individual wants the data and information "forgotten" after a period of time (Preliminary question 3).

Of these, preliminary questions 2 and 3 are more directly connected with our subject of study. In opposition to the request to delete links to the web sites collected among the search results, Google submitted to the Spanish National High Court that:

> N. 63: by virtue of the principle of proportionality, any request seeking the removal of information must be addressed to the publisher of the website concerned because it is they who takes the responsibility for making the information public, who are in a position to appraise the lawfulness of that publication and who has available to them the most effective and least restrictive means of making the information inaccessible. Furthermore, to require the operator of a search engine to withdraw information published on the internet from its indexes would take insufficient account of the fundamental rights of publishers of websites, of other internet users and of that operator itself.[1]

Nevertheless, the European Court of Justice interpreted that the directive on Data Protection requires the manager of the search engine to take responsibility for the processing of personal data involved in its service:

> N. 72: (art. 6 Directive of Data Protection) Under Article 6 of Directive 95/46 and without prejudice to specific provisions that the Member States may lay down in respect of processing for historical, statistical or scientific purposes, the controller has the task of ensuring that personal data is processed 'fairly and lawfully', that it is 'collected for specified, explicit and legitimate purposes and not further processed in a way incompatible with those purposes', that it is 'adequate, relevant and not excessive in relation to the purposes for which they are collected and/or further processed', that it is 'accurate and, where necessary, kept up to date'.

As a consequence, it was determined that a user can address a request to delete personal data from a website towards the search engine:

> N. 77: Requests under Article 12(b) and subparagraph (a) of the first paragraph of Article 14 of Directive 95/46 may be addressed by the data subject directly to the controller who must then duly examine their merits and, as the case may be, end processing of the data in question. Where the controller does not grant the request, the data subject may bring the matter before the supervisory authority or the judicial authority (. . .)

The Spanish National High Court also raised in its third preliminary question:

> N. 83: Can the interpretation of Article 12(b) and subparagraph (a) of the first paragraph of Article 14 of Directive 95/46 be that which enables the data subject to require the operator of a search engine to remove from the list of results [. . .] on the ground that that information may be prejudicial to them or that they wish it to be 'forgotten' after a certain time? (Preliminary question 3).

---

[1]Judgment of the Court (Grand Chamber) of 13 May 2014 Google Spain SL and Google Inc. v. Agencia Española de Protección de Datos (AEPD) and Mario Coseja González (Case C-131/12) ECLI:EU:C:2014:317) or (Case C-131/12, 13 May 2014 Google Spain SL and Google Inc. v. Agencia Española de Protección de Datos (AEPD) and Mario Costeja González.

Google had said that, in these last circumstances, the deletion of the links from the search results cannot be requested, because it is not logical that the simple will of forgetting information about a person justifies the duty of the search engine to delete it:

> N. 90: [...] confer rights upon data subjects only if the processing in question is incompatible with the directive or on compelling legitimate grounds relating to their particular situation and not merely because they consider that that processing may be prejudicial to them or they wish that the data being processed sink into oblivion.

On the contrary, the European Court of Justice insisted that it is possible to oblige the search engine to delete these contents, because:

> N. 93: even initially lawful processing of accurate data may, in the course of time, become incompatible with the directive where the data is no longer necessary in the light of the purposes for which it was collected or processed. This is particularly so where it appears to be inadequate, irrelevant or no longer relevant, or excessive in relation to those purposes and in the light of the time that has elapsed.

This means that requests for the deletion of personal data should be resolved on a case by case basis, taking into consideration the criteria mentioned by this decision and the European legislation, relating to the exactitude, adequacy, relevance—including the elapsed time—and the proportionality of the links in relation to personal data processing (Cfr. N. 93).

4.3 Balancing Rights in the Application of the Right to Be Forgotten

Following the text of the decision of the European Court of Justice in the case Mario Costeja v. Google, the examination of proportionality among the rights which ask for the deletion of the search results (privacy and personal data) and those which protect the economic benefit derived from data processing, as well as the satisfaction of interest of the public for the access to information, the opinion of the European Court of Justice is the absolute prevalence of the fundamental rights:

> N. 99: As the data subject may, in the light of their fundamental rights under Articles 7 and 8 of the Charter, request that the information in question no longer be made available to the general public on account of its inclusion in such a list of results, those rights override, as a rule, not only the economic interest of the operator of the search engine but also the interest of the general public in having access to that information upon a search relating to the data subject's name.

In circumstances where the individuals—because of their activities or personalities—have a public profile, the possibility to request of the search engine to delete personal data is much more limited:

> N. 99: However, that would not be the case if it appeared, for particular reasons, such as the role played by the data subject in public life, that interference with their fundamental rights

is justified by the preponderant interest of the general public in having, on account of its inclusion in the list of results, access to the information in question.

In any case, due to the certainty of the statement it is surprising that the right to privacy and the right to the protection of personal data take precedence over the public's right to have access to all information on the internet. This is especially interesting since the constitutional jurisprudence of the majority of European countries, Spain among them, has chosen to examine on a case by case basis the criteria in cases of conflict between the right to information and freedom of expression and the rights of reputation, privacy and self-image, all without having established the precedence of one right over the others. In some way, the decision of the European Court of Justice in this case builds a defence of privacy against a new dimension of risk generated by the internet and search engines. This danger affects not only celebrities and public persons, but all individuals. Citizens can therefore see that there are thousands of internet pages linked to their names. These include pictures of individuals, captured and spread on the internet by third parties; pictures from private lives or from public situations, recent or from the past; content with personal references in official newspapers—all of which are available online today—including a diversity of professional or legal topics related to that particular person; and also in any digital newspaper or blog, recently published or, conversely, published many years ago, etc., including home addresses, telephone numbers, email accounts, commentaries by third persons involving personal issues, and a long list of possibilities of damage to privacy. Some content is registered on a second level by the companies operating the internet—content which is connected to tastes, habits, hobbies and addictions. There are also unsolved issues such as the possibility that, once personal data is deleted from a search index, the normal activity of search engines can lead to the data being indexed again (Artemi 2014). This can also occur if a search is made not by a person's name but by other criteria, such as an offensive or insulting word which leads to search results connected to the person's name (Buisán García 2014). Also, it is necessary to determine the criteria that balance interests more narrowly to make it easier for search engines to face requests for the right to be forgotten (Mieres Mieres 2014). The European Court of Justice has chosen to place the right to be forgotten as one of the elements of the right of informational self-determination. Andrés Boix Palop observed that the right to be forgotten

is not a derivation of the privacy guarantees, but a consequence of the idea of (Autodeterminación Informativa) informative self-determination (art. 18.4 Spanish Constitution and art. 8 of the Bill of Rights of the European Union), and therefore, this right has a different profile to the other rights of personality set by art. 18 of the Spanish Constitution (the right to privacy and right to protection of personal data), rights which, in some ways, have been shaped, legally speaking, by the regulations on data protection. There are consequences arising from this, especially in the relationship between these rights and freedom of expression (Boix Palop 2015).

In any case, the decision of the European Court of Justice represents an important push in the current reform of personal data, in which the court wanted the "right to be forgotten" to be included. Remarkably, as Andrés Boix Palop points out, "beyond the existing dogmatic constructions of the 'right to be forgotten' it is important to say that, as from the 'Google Decision' of the European Court of Justice, this right is now recognised by European Law as a true right" (Boix Palop 2015).

5 The Application of the Sentence of the European Court of Justice on Google v Spain by the Decision of December 29, 2014 Taken by the Audiencia Nacional (National High Court)

The Administrative Chamber of the National High Court finally decided the Mario Costeja case in its decision of December 29, 2014, published January 23, 2015, to which the arguments of the European Court of Justice's decision of May 13, 2014, were applied. It was the first time that a Spanish court recognised the right to be forgotten, and at the same time this decision set the criteria for balancing possible conflicts. The right to be forgotten was described as a "personal power of decision over a person's own data published on the internet" (Fundamento de Derecho 13. Criteria for balancing). It is a definition in line with the one which the National High Court presented to the European Court of Justice in its third preliminary question which asked whether a citizen has the right to directly request of the search engines to end the indexation of personal information. "It is a request based on the personal will to keep this information inaccessible, when the person concerned considers that knowledge of this information can damage them or wants to forget the information". (Fundamento de Derecho 13. Criteria for balancing) It is an individual's decision whether information should remain accessible on the internet. In respecting this right, the search engines are obliged to de-index undesired content. As the Spanish National High Court has said: it is a "personal power of disposition" (Fundamento de Derecho 13. Criteria for balancing). Google fought this idea, saying that it wasn't logical that the mere will of a person could justify the duty of the search engine to delete personal data. From Google's point of view, this can be justified only if the personal data processing were incompatible with the directive or if there were legitimate reasons resulting from the particular situation of the person in question. The European Court of Justice has pointed out that it is not possible to take only incompatibility with the directive on personal data protection into account when considering a person's right to request the deletion of personal data. The main circumstance which must be taken into account is the effect of the time elapsed. Therefore, it is possible that something which was legitimately published by a newspaper or website can become "inadequate, irrelevant or no longer relevant, or excessive in proportion with the aims of these personal data processed" (N. 93 Google Spain SL and Google Inc. v. Agencia Española de Protección de Datos (AEPD) and Mario Costeja González) in the context of the search engine activity. This means that incompatibility with the law is no longer a solid criterion that can serve as the grounds for this personal prerogative facing internet search engines. It will be necessary to go beyond legal texts and to create a balance in order to know definitively whether accessibility to personal data is or is not compatible with the directive. Taking into account the definition of the "right to be forgotten", the decision of the Spanish National High Court has confirmed what the European Court of Justice pointed out in its answers to the preliminary consultation made by the Spanish Court:

1. The search engine can be obliged to de-index a list of search results linked to the name of a person, even if the initial diffusion of this information was legitimate:

   The manager of a search engine is obliged to delete from the list of search results obtained after a search via the name of a person, links to web sites that have been published by third parties and which contain information related to this person; and also in the case that this name or the personal information haven't been deleted previously or simultaneously in these web sites, and, even, if the publication in these pages is essentially licit (Fundamento de Derecho 13- Criteria of Balancing).

2. It is not necessary that the accessibility of the personal information causes prejudice to the person concerned, for the application of the "right to be forgotten", because:

   The right to privacy and the protection of personal data (art. 7 and 8 European Union Charter of Rights) prevails, in principle, not only upon the economic power of the manager of the search engine, but over the interest of the public to access the above-mentioned information, in a search by the name of this person", with the exception of the case where there is somebody who has a role in public life or a similar circumstance. In this last case, "the trespass on their fundamental rights would be justified due to a preponderant interest of the public in having access to this information (. . .) (cf. Fundamento de Derecho 13.- Criteria of balancing).

The Spanish National High Court formed an interpretation of the arguments of the European Court of Justice decision based mainly on those principles and criteria which are applicable to the facts that are judged. Those are the need to balance the rights in conflict; the consideration of the relevance of the criteria of the time elapsed; the need for a fair balance between the legitimate interest of internet users to access information; and the rights of a person concerned by this information. This is a balance that depends on "the nature of the information, the sensitive character of the information towards the intimacy of the person concerned, and the interest of the audience in having this information" and that "can vary depending on the role that this particular person plays in public life" (Fundamento de Derecho 13.- Criteria of balancing). The outcome of balancing different interests can also be different depending on whether the processing was made by a search engine, in origin or by a website.

It is noteworthy that the decision of the Spanish National High Court follows the procedure set by the European Court of Justice by which one can make a request to the manager of data processing to delete the information and, if they don't respond, that the request can be addressed to the data authority or to the courts. There is one regard, however, in which the Spanish Court goes beyond the arguments of the

European Court of Justice, in the sense that the prevalence of the protection of personal data cannot be understood as an absolute right, under any criteria:

> (...) from the Decision (of the European Court of Justice) a prevalence of the right of personal data protection (....) is deduced. However, this prevalence of the right to oppose the data processing by its holder upon the legitimate interest of the manager of a search engine is neither absolute nor alien to the particular personal situation of the claimant, with the only exception that the law could set a different provision. The protection of personal data is one example of the protection of the fundamental right to privacy. However, it may be justified to interfere with and limit that right when, as provided by law, such interference or limitation is considered a necessary measure in a democratic society to safeguard other interests, including the protection of the rights and freedoms of others, as established in Art. 8 of the European Convention on Human Rights of 4 November 1950 and in Art. 52.1 and 52.3 of the European Charter (Fundamento de Derecho 13.- Criteria of balancing).

6 Conclusion

The right to be forgotten—as recently approved by the European Court of Justice in the Decision of May 2014 and as the Spanish National High Court applied it in the Decision of December 2014—allows that personal information disseminated on the internet by search engines, and therefore out of the concerned person's control, may be deleted if the concerned person demands so. This right can be applied if the following conditions expressed by the European Court of Justice are present: the data must be "inadequate, irrelevant or no longer relevant, or excessive in relation to those purposes towards which the data processing was aimed" (N. 93 Case C-131/12, 13 May 2014 Google Spain SL and Google Inc. v. Agencia Española de Protección de Datos (AEPD) and Mario Costeja González). If the indexation of someone's personal data is performed by a company based in Spain, it will be balanced with the freedom of expression and the right to information following the balancing criteria set by the Spanish Constitutional Court. The right to personal data protection is, in principle, dependent upon the economic interests of the managers of search engines and upon the citizens' right to access this data on the internet. The right to informational self-determination is currently gaining ground in European legislation. It offers a formulation of data protection rights that is better suited to the reality of an information society.

As a more concrete result, the decision of the European Court of Justice has established a means to resolve conflicts between citizens and search engines. This is possible thanks to the right of every person to ask the manager of the search engine for the deletion of their data when it is "inadequate, irrelevant or no longer relevant" (N. 93 Case C-131/12, 13 May 2014 Google Spain SL and Google Inc. v. Agencia Española de Protección de Datos (AEPD) and Mario Coseja González) under the control of the proper authorities, and, in particular, of the Data Protection Authorities. Eight months after the publication of the decision of the European Court of Justice, the news agency Reuters reported 200,000 submissions for the deletion of internet links in Europe, which would affect around 700,000 URLs.

References

Artemi, R. (2014). *El derecho al olvido en Internet. Google versus España*. Madrid: Centro de Estudios Políticos y Constitucionales.

Boix Palop, A. (2015). El equilibrio entre los derechos del artículo 18 de la Constitución, el «Derecho al olvido» y las libertades informativas tras la sentencia Google. *Revista General de Derecho Administrativo, 38*, 1–40.

Buisán García, N. (2014). El derecho al olvido. *El Cronista del Estado Social y Democrático de Derecho, 46*, 22–35.

Cotino Hueso, L. (2015) El conflicto entre las libertades de expresión e información en Internet y el derecho a la protección de datos. El derecho al olvido y sus retos: un falso derecho a juzgar por un falso tribunal. Bel Mallén, I. y Corredoira Alfonso, L. *Derecho de la Información. Derecho de la Información y su Jurisprudencia* (pp. 339–388). Madrid: Centro de Estudios Constitucionales y Políticos.

De la Valgoma, M. (1983). Comentario a la ley orgánica de protección civil del derecho al honor, a la intimidad familiar y personal y a la propia imagen. *Anuario de Derechos Humanos* (2), 652.

Díez Picazo, J. L. (1979). *Estudios sobre Jurisprudencia Civi*. Madrid: Tecnos.

Herrero Tejedor, F. (1990). *Honor, Intimidad e Imagen*. Madrid: Colex.

Mieres Mieres, L. J. (2014). *El derecho al olvido digital. Resumen ejecutivo*. Madrid: Laboratorio Alternativas.

Pérez Fuertes, G. M. (2004). Evolución Doctrinal, Legislativa y Jurisprudencial de los derechos de la personalidad y el daño moral en España. *Revista de Derecho Privado* (8), 111–146.

Tene, O. (2011). Privacy: The new generations. *International Data Privacy Law, 1*(1), 15–27.

Voss, G. (2014). The right to be forgotten in the European Union: Enforcement in the court of justice and amendment to the proposed general data protection in regulation. *Journal of Internet Law, 18*, 3–7.

Harvesting Social Media for Journalistic Purposes in the UK

The Balance Between Privacy Rights and Freedom of Expression

Bernhard Gross

1 Introduction

A journalist working for a national newspaper in London goes through recent postings of viral videos on Facebook. She comes across one that allegedly shows a rat running across the parking lot of a fast food restaurant. The video also shows an employee of the restaurant behind the counter of the drive-through window and the customer who filmed the alleged rat encounter demanding his money back. The journalist writes an online story about the video and hyperlinks it. This scenario is based on real events and highlights why social media is a goldmine for journalists. Always available and only a couple of keystrokes or search terms away, Twitter, Facebook and YouTube offer an abundance of information, comments, pictures and videos. Story ideas, story bits and pieces as well as entire stories await, ripe for the picking. No need to make a phone call or go to meetings. A bit of copying and pasting and—presto—there is another article. Well, not that fast. This may be how it seems, but in reality the situation is more complex. Take the example above: a few days after the journalist posted the story, her company received notice from its regulator that a complaint had been made about the video. For journalists, social media can often feel like a goldmine in the middle of a minefield.

An important aspect is the issue of reliability and truth. Not everything that is posted on social media is necessarily what it claims to be. Is this a disparaging tweet from the mayor about the leader of the city council opposition or is it a post from a fake account? Does this video really show a rat running across the parking lot of a fast food restaurant in a city a couple of hours up the motorway? Was this video really shot yesterday and not 2 years ago? Verification, the process of finding the right answers to these questions, can be challenging, and journalists can get it

B. Gross (✉)
The University of the West of England, Bristol, UK
e-mail: Bernhard.Gross@uwe.ac.uk

© Springer International Publishing AG 2017
W.J. Schünemann, M.-O. Baumann (eds.), *Privacy, Data Protection and Cybersecurity in Europe*, DOI 10.1007/978-3-319-53634-7_3

wrong. More importantly for this chapter, there are also laws, regulations and guidelines that shape and influence how journalists can draw on social media. Taking laws and regulations into account requires a shift of focus from generic journalistic practice—that is, the things journalists might do regardless of where they work—to how journalists operate in a particular country with its specific legal and regulatory contexts—in the case of this chapter, the UK. An obvious example would be the allocation of copyright. While there are some international legal frameworks that shape this issue globally and which journalists around the world must consider, there are also national laws that differ from one another. Journalists in different places, say, in the UK and in Germany, must consider the nuances of the law as it applies to them. And although copyright is from a different field, that of legal ownership and distribution rights, it is in many ways similar to verification. Establishing copyrights may be challenging, but it ultimately leads to clear answers within a specific legal context—at least in most cases in the context of journalism. Privacy, the focus of this chapter, is less clear cut.

The issue of privacy raises the question of whether and under which circumstances a journalist *can* as well as *should* use a tweet, YouTube video, Facebook post or other social media content. In some cases, there is a simple answer. For instance, when young children are involved, the answer will usually be a "no, do not use it". Most cases, though, are not as straightforward. Just because a piece of social media content is online, accessible and not protected by copyright, does not necessarily suffice as a justification for a journalist to use it, although it might. The law in the UK, as far as it exists at all, allows for a wide range of interpretations and arguments. It is based on the balancing of two fundamental human rights derived from the European Convention on Human Rights (Council Europe 1950) and enshrined in UK law by the Human Rights Act (HM Government 1998). Article 8 of the Act outlines the *Right to respect for private and family life* and Article 10 the *Right to freedom of expression*. Someone on the receiving end of an alleged press intrusion into his or her private life in the UK cannot sue for breach or invasion of privacy because no such law exists. Instead, a number of alternative legal claims have been used in UK courts to approximate the breach of privacy in absence of such a law. If a plaintiff wants to file a case on the breach of privacy, the claim must be based on an infringement of human rights. Journalists justify compromising *someone's* human right to private and family life on the basis of the human right to freedom of expression. In court these competing claims need to be weighed against one another. In the English Common Law system, decisions made by the courts on a case can set precedents against which future cases are judged. Over the course of the last 20 years, since the introduction of the Human Rights Act, the courts have issued a series of judgements that have shaped the legal understanding of privacy. However, these decisions still ultimately rest on the balancing of two fundamental human rights and are not enshrined in statutory law.

Things become more specific when moving from the legal to the regulatory context within which journalists operate in the UK. This regulatory context consists of various regulatory frameworks specific to different sections of the journalism industry. In the British regulatory system, it matters whether a journalist works in the broadcasting sector or for a newspaper; in fact, it may matter for which newspaper a journalist writes. Thus, at the same time as making the issue of privacy more specific, the move to the regulatory context recalls the range of interpretations and arguments brought up by the national legal context in the UK. The aim of this chapter is to unravel some of these complexities on the regulatory level by comparing the positions and considerations established through the Editors' Code of Practice (2015, 2016), the Ofcom Broadcasting Code (2015) and the BBC's Editorial Guidelines (2015b). The focus will be on the Editors Code of Practice in a domestic, local journalism context rather than on national, foreign or international journalism. There is a substantive body of research on journalistic practices around social media in political, national and international contexts, such as Hermida et al.'s (2014) study of the Arab Spring. Many of these studies have highlighted, on the one hand, the positive impact journalists' use of social media has on widening public debate and political discourse; they even suggest that social media has contributed to the overthrow of repressive regimes. The local level, on the other hand, has received scant attention. It is important to make this distinction, as this kind of journalism engages more frequently with ordinary people and their day-to-day activities. By taking a closer look at two cases decided upon by a journalism regulator, emerging discourses on privacy and journalistic use of social media in domestic and local situations will be highlighted. To provide the necessary context in an interdisciplinary publication such as this, some key issues closely related to this topic from the field of journalism studies must be outlined at the outset. This overview will show the importance of the debate on emerging practises that deal with challenges in digital media. The role of journalism in society, the relationship between journalists and their sources, and the influence social media has on journalism will all be looked at. Any field of study naturally has its own subfields, debates and disagreements. This overview cannot fully capture the diversity of the field. Rather, its aim is to establish the position from which the central issue of this chapter will be explored. The same applies to the second contextual section, which will provide a brief overview of media regulation in the UK. Not only is the situation complex, it is also very contentious and therefore under continuous construction. Again, the aim of that section is to offer a snapshot to aid understanding, not a comprehensive consideration of the nuances of the debate.

2 From the Role of Journalism in Society to the Disappearance of Journalism in the Digital Age

In this chapter, journalism has been referred to almost as though the term needed no further explanation or definition—as if there were only one kind of journalism, differentiated into local, national and international. In fact, journalism comprises a wide spectrum of genres, formats and media. The journalism referred to in this chapter is the kind of journalism that supports the exchange of ideas necessary for development and progress in liberal, democratic societies. Habermasian conceptualisations of the public sphere serve as a good reference point to a deeper understanding. Summarising Habermas's ideas, Curran highlights the central role of mass media in the public sphere, claiming that "they enable the people to shape the conduct of government by articulating their views. The media are thus the principal institutions of the public sphere or, in the rhetoric of nineteenth-century liberalism, 'the fourth estate of the realm'" (1991: 29). In the age of mass media, journalism still occupies this fourth estate role, holding not just governments but also other powerful interests and institutions accountable to the public. Journalists shape social norms by covering everyday events and issues that range from church fetes, coronations, court cases and football games to migration, gender rights and race relations.

Daily newspapers, weekly or monthly news magazines as well as radio and television news and current affairs programmes have been the dominant formats of this genre of journalism in the post-World-War-II period, at least until recently. Online forms of communication have presented an ever-increasing challenge to this dominance since their emergence in the media mainstream in the 1990s. New online formats have emerged and continue to develop. Today, a newspaper's website or a link to an article posted on social media attract more readers than the print version. New media formats and forms of distribution have challenged the business models which used to fund professional journalism. Moreover, the public now has access to alternative media content from that provided by professional journalists. The fact that almost anybody with internet access can disseminate information has called professional journalism's position as the central fourth estate institution in the public sphere into question. Yet professional journalism has, though under pressure, managed to maintain the dominant position for the time being. The key questions of journalism studies are to which degree journalism lives up to the fourth estate role and whether it claims a central position in informing the public.

One particular focus of analysis is the relationship between journalists and their sources. Gans argues in one of the first detailed ethnographic studies of newsroom practices that this relationship "resembles a dance, for sources seek access to journalists, and journalists seek access to sources. Although it takes two to tango, either sources or journalists can lead" (1979: 116). The dance metaphor highlights that the journalist-source relationship involves fluctuating power relations, a struggle over the lead, and possibly even a reluctance to join in the dance. For Broersma et al., it is this dynamic that defines not only journalism but also the *public* sphere: "Journalism is in essence a struggle over the boundaries of the public sphere; a struggle over what information becomes public and what remains in the private realm, and which topics are discussed openly and which remain concealed" (2013: 388). Analysing the forces that shape the journalism-source relationship allows for an understanding of whether journalism fulfils its fourth estate role and if so, to what extent and in which situations. At times journalists wield power, and at times they are at the receiving end of it. In either case, this may be to the benefit or to the detriment of the public sphere.

As Gans's dance metaphor points out, the relationship depends on the context and the situation. A live interview on national television has a different power dynamic than an interview for print conducted in person or over the phone. More specifically, an interview with a politician announcing the successful rescue of hostages differs from an interview with the same politician under pressure for an election scandal. It also matters whether the interviewee is indeed an elite or prominent source, such as a politician or celebrity, or not. The latter distinction highlights how laws and regulations prescribe the overall context *as well as* the specific situation, a point to be developed further in the next section. Two further aspects pertaining to context and linking back to the idea of social media as goldmine need mentioning first: the promise of social media to (a) solve logistical challenges and (b) improve the public sphere. Writing in the late 1970s, Gans identifies logistics as a key determinant of the journalist-source relationship and discusses the impact this has on the public sphere: "Staff and time being in short supply, journalists actively pursue only a small number of regular sources who have been available and suitable in the past, and are passive toward other possible news sources" (1979: 116). Logistical constraints lead to a limited range of voices and, consequently, to a limited and possibly distorted debate in the public sphere. It is important to consider this not only in the context of political debate but also in the context of the selection and coverage of everyday events. Frequency and coverage perspective highlight and shape which content is considered normal, extraordinary or deviant. The easy accessibility of a broad range of sources via social media thus has not only the potential to answer the logistical challenge, but such "an approach to reporting could be considered as a more representative form of journalism, addressing concerns about an overreliance on powerful, institutional elites as sourcing" (Hermida et al. 2014: 493). However, this potential should be considered in the context of the challenges facing the journalism industry since the emergence of online and social media outlined above. Compared to the late 1970s, when Gans conducted his studies, "Reporters have fewer resources and less time to write more stories" (Broersma and Graham 2013: 447). Consequently, the way journalists *actually use* social media may fall short of the potential of social media in terms of answering the challenges of logistics and widening participation.

3 Media Regulation in the UK: A Developing Situation

The situation of media regulation in the UK is complex and still being established. Its overall set up is shaped by a differentiation between print and broadcast journalism. Unregulated during the early and middle parts of the twentieth century, the print sector has developed forms of self-regulation over recent decades. The broadcast sector, on the other hand, has a history of more direct regulation by the state. State regulation should not be confused with state control; its aim is to ensure a diversity of broadcast services. In the public debate of the issue, any regulation of the news media is perceived as a potential threat to press freedom. In the case of broadcasting, specific arguments have been made to justify such regulation. Among others, signal scarcity is one of the key justifications. Because only a limited number of channels can be run on the broadcasting signal, the state must regulate to ensure a plurality of voices across broadcasting. The wider and more intrusive reach of the broadcast signal compared to the limitations of print media distribution has been put forward as another key argument for closer regulation of the sector. The Office of Communications, commonly known as Ofcom, currently regulates the commercial broadcast sector as well as some aspects of the BBC. At the time of writing this chapter, the BBC is mainly regulated by the BBC Trust. This may change with the upcoming renewal of the Royal Charter, which defines the institutional organization of the BBC. The current pre-settlement debate suggests that the BBC Trust may give up power, letting Ofcom take over regulation of the BBC in all its aspects.

For the print sector the issue of signal scarcity does not apply, and any intervention from the state has been branded a clampdown on press freedom. To address concerns over print journalists abusing their freedom, the sector has attempted to self-regulate and set up several institutions to this purpose over the years. The most recent regulatory body, the Press Complaints Commission, collapsed in the wake of the so-called Phone Hacking Scandal[1]. The Leveson Inquiry, an official inquiry into the scandal and the regulation of the press, concluded in late 2012 that a new press regulator should be supported by a Royal Charter. Like the institutional arrangements for the BBC, this set-up is meant to prevent undue government influence on the press and thus, in theory, ensure improved regulation of the press without a negative impact on press freedom. After some delay, Impress, a chartered press regulator, became operational in 2016. However, some newspaper publishers have remained suspicious of this arrangement. Instead they continue to use the Independent Press Standards Organisation (IPSO), an unchartered regulator set up in 2014.

Consequently, some publishers are regulated by a non-sanctioned regulator and other publishers are not regulated at all. One aspect that should become apparent in all of this is that these regulatory arrangements do not adequately take the current journalistic landscape into account. The argument over signal scarcity has survived the emergence of satellite and cable, but in the era of internet protocol television (IPTV) and YouTube it appears increasingly hollow. The same could be said for reach, with newspaper publishers running ever more sophisticated websites that are not limited by the format of print publications. And yet, this is the situation journalists in the UK currently face. While the law is the same for everyone, different rules apply depending on what kind of media outlet a journalist works for. The next section will briefly look at how privacy is considered in the *Ofcom Broadcasting*

---

[1] As the name suggests, the scandal involved the hacking of voicemail messages by or on behalf of journalists. Targeted were not only celebrities and other people in the public eye but also victims of crime.

Code (2015) and the Editors' Code of Practice (2016), which IPSO draws on to adjudicate cases. The application of the Editors' Code will then be discussed in relation to two cases adjudicated by IPSO. In the final section, the BBC's *Editorial Guidelines* (2015b) will be drawn upon to highlight the contingency of media regulations in a swiftly changing media environment.

4   Privacy and Its Intersection with Social Media in UK Media Regulation

Section 8 of the Ofcom Code (2015) focusses on privacy. The governing principle is "to ensure that broadcasters avoid any unwarranted infringement of privacy in programmes and in connection with obtaining material included in programmes." Rule 8.1 defines the key consideration when applying the principle: "Any infringement of privacy in programmes, or in connection with obtaining material included in programmes, must be warranted." In a brief explanation of the specific meaning of the term "unwarranted", public interest is singled out as a possible argument. However, in a defence based on public interest "the broadcaster should be able to demonstrate that the public interest outweighs the right to privacy." What follows are 21 *Practices to be followed* articles (8.2–8.22). Over the course of six pages these articles define practices around issues such as requiring consent, the use of surreptitious filming or under what circumstances the practice of door stepping may be warranted. Although structured differently, the Editors' Code of Practice (2016)[2] echoes the concerns of Section 8 of the Ofcom Code, particularly in terms of balancing privacy against public interest and the need to *demonstrate* public interest rather than merely claim it. Both codes stress "legitimate" (Ofcom) or "reasonable" (Editors' Code) expectations of privacy in public and private places as well as consent from sources in general. However, they also highlight that consideration should be given to the extent to which information is already publicly available. The Editors' Code also puts explicit emphasis on the human rights dimension of public interest by stating that "there is a public interest in freedom of expression itself." Neither code explicitly addresses social media, though the Editors' Code mentions respect for everyone's "correspondence, including digital communications" in the section on privacy. Looking at two recent cases decided on by IPSO will provide some insight into how this may apply in practice.[3]

---

[2]It should be noted that at the time of writing this chapter, in January 2016, the Editors' Code of Practice Committee implemented a revised version of the code. Roy Greenslade (2015), a former newspaper editor and one of the leading media observers in the UK, commented upon its publication that the "new code . . . is anything but a root-and-branch revision. It should be seen instead as another stage in the code's evolution since it was first drafted in 1990."

[3]These examples serve to illustrate emerging arguments over the balance between privacy and freedom of expression in a social media context. They do not represent a systematic review of IPSO's decisions in this field. Also, these decisions were based on the previous, the 2015 version of

The first case takes us back to the rat in the parking lot. In Rainford v Mirror.co. uk (2015a), the father of the 16-year-old girl working for the fast food restaurant made a complaint. The father claimed that his daughter had not given consent to being filmed and claimed that, though his daughter had not been named, she had been recognised locally and had suffered abuse because of the article. He argued that the article had breached three clauses of the code in relation to privacy, harassment and the treatment of children. IPSO rejected all complaints. The issue of the treatment of children is of course important in general but of less relevance here, as the code is rather straightforward on this issue. Outside of school, the clause only applies to children younger than 16. As the daughter was not filmed at school, the rule did not apply. IPSO's argument for rejecting the complaint elaborates on the specific situation in which the filming took place. It deals with two aspects: the customer's right to make the video and the journalist's right to use it. The regulator stated that the daughter was in a "public place, visible from the car park, and she was not engaged in any private activity." This shows that privacy rights cannot be expected to apply in a public space when carrying out a public activity. This justifies the making of the video. The consideration of the customer's actions is somewhat surprising as the explanation continues in relation to the journalist's use of the video: "Furthermore, the video was already in the public domain on social media when the newspaper published the article on its website. The newspaper had not disclosed any private information about the complainant's daughter." This explanation recalls the characterisation of social media as a goldmine made at the beginning of this chapter. The video is already out there, is already public, so it is fair game. However, the fact that IPSO also considered the making of the video is important to keep in mind, a point that will be discussed in relation to IPSO's decision on the harassment complaint.

IPSO's rejection of the harassment complaint deserves a closer look because it introduces an important aspect of journalistic responsibility in the use of social media content. Per the clause on harassment in the Editors' Code (2015), "(i) Journalists must not engage in intimidation, harassment or persistent pursuit. (ii) They must not persist in questioning, telephoning, pursuing or photographing individuals once asked to desist". This definition implicitly contains a notion of privacy. Harassment can be defined as an unwarranted and sustained invasion of someone's privacy against his or her expressed wishes to stop the invasion. IPSO rejected the harassment complaint on the basis that the terms of the clause "generally relate to the conduct of journalists during the newsgathering process. Although the complainant's daughter had not consented to being filmed, she did not request that the customer desist from filming. In response to him saying that he was 'free to record' her, she had replied 'what when I've not given permission'" (Rainsford v Mirror.co.uk 2015a). The wording suggests that IPSO placed emphasis on the fact

---

the Editors' Code of Practice. Considering the changes and Greenslade's assessment of them (see previous footnote), it is unlikely that the decision would have differed, if the 2016 version had applied.

that the daughter had not clearly stated that she did not want to be filmed and merely posed a hypothetical question about consent or the lack of it. More interestingly, by ruling on this issue IPSO seemed to accept that the customer who made the film was acting in a quasi-journalistic role and to suggest that professional journalists who use this kind of social media content need to apply the code to the original quasi-newsgathering process. The actions of regular people like the customer are not IPSO's concern, as they only have jurisdiction over the conduct of professional journalists. Only when such material is used by journalists working for a publisher covered by IPSO do questions over the creation of such content arise. The use of material in the public domain created by a third party does not absolve professional journalists from applying their professional code of conduct. In this case, had the daughter explicitly asked the customer to stop filming, the journalist may not have been in a position to use the video.[4]

In the case of Rainford v Mirror.co.uk the issue of public domain was considered in the context of third party content; the journalist used content created by someone else, the customer, about someone else, the fast-food restaurant employee. The former explicitly wanted the content to gain public attention. According to the article on the Mirror website, the customer posted the video on Facebook with the comment: "Attention, don't go to Burger King in St Helens has a MAJOR RAT PROBLEM......!!!!! Just been now and I think the girl refused to see the rat less than 3 feet away from me...... PLEASE SHARE.....!!!!" (O'Neill 2015). While, in this case, the person posting intended to reach a wider public, the situation in the case of Johnson v Dartmouth Chronicle (2015b) is different. Not all details of the case are relevant here. It involves the engagement of a journalist with an official of a local business improvement district on the official's *private* Facebook account as well as using posts from her *private* Facebook account at an earlier stage.[5] In relation to the latter aspect of the case, IPSO considered whether privacy had been breached. The committee rejected the claim with the explanation that "The newspaper had reported separate comments the complainant had posted on her Facebook page, which, at the time, was open to the public. The comments were already in the public domain; the newspaper had not disclosed private information about the complainant in breach of Clause 3." Again, it is the public domain argument that is drawn on here. However, in this case the content is not explicitly identified for further dissemination as was the case with the rat video. In the second case the content was simply publicly accessible. In its verdict IPSO uses, almost verbatim, the same explanation and makes no distinction between the two situations.

---

[4]This sentence must be qualified by 'may', as other arguments could have been put forward that would have warranted publication, for instance a public interest defence based on public health concerns.

[5]In this instance private account refers to a Facebook account not associated with her work. The privacy settings of this private account allowed for the account to be accessed openly. Only after the events did the woman change her settings to more limited, "Friends only" access level.

5 Conclusion and Outlook

The differing circumstances regarding the intended audience of the information in these cases suggest that a distinction should have or at least could have been made. First, there is the question of whether social media users understand the privacy settings of their accounts. Watson et al. summarise various surveys of end-users that "have shown an increase in the awareness and modification of Facebook privacy settings over the years, yet many users still do not seem to be familiar with the extent of the privacy settings on Facebook or take the time to configure all possible settings" (2015: 32.2). While the Editors' Code of Practice and IPSO's adjudications do not appear to consider this issue and thereby hold social media users fully responsible for their settings, the more detailed BBC Editorial Guidelines outline a more nuanced approach. Under 7.4.8 *Material from Social Media*, a subsection of the *Privacy and Informed Consent* section, the guidelines qualify the public domain. "Although material, especially pictures and videos, on third party social media and other websites where the public have ready access may be considered to have been placed in the public domain, re-use by the BBC will usually bring it to a much wider audience. We should consider the impact of our re-use..." (BBC 2015b). In addition, further guidance on *Pictures from Social Media* raises a question that shifts the key consideration from one of availability to one of intent. "What was the original intention in publication? The publication of a picture on a personal website or social networking site does not necessarily mean the owner of that picture intended it to be available for all purposes and circumstances—or understood that it could be" (BBC 2015a). Both the guidelines and the additional guidance single out situations of grief and trauma when these considerations become particularly pertinent, but they are also clear on the fact that they are not restricted to such situations.

With their emphasis on intent and reach, the BBC guidelines and guidance reimagine the public domain not as one undifferentiated open space where the release of information in one spot implies that it can be taken and disseminated. Instead, it is seen as one bounded by reach and intent—at least these aspects ought to find consideration. Jeff Jarvis, one of the most influential commentators on developments in contemporary media and journalism, echoes this idea especially in relation to intent when writing about the "private publics" of social media. Referring to Facebook and its founder Mark Zuckerberg and the social network's ever changing privacy settings, Jarvis suggests that they "seem to assume that once something is public, it's public. ... But when I put something on Facebook my assumption had been that I was sharing it just with the public I created and control there. *That public is private*" (2010, original emphasis). At the same time, it is difficult to make assumptions about a specific user's intentions. Swigger observed generational differences in terms of privacy attitudes. He argues that users on social networking sites "become accustomed to a world where privacy is an afterthought, ... Self-publicizing activity seems to create citizens with different value priorities than those who matured before the internet became such a widespread tool" (2013:

599). Data from Eurobarometer (2015) appears to bear out Swigger's argument. Seven out of ten persons aged 15–24 tried to change their privacy settings, while only half as many persons aged over 55 did the same.

While the focus of this chapter has been on domestic news in the UK, it is also important to highlight that privacy attitudes and practices differ between countries. The BBC Guidance does take account of changing attitudes, not just in generational terms but also in terms of society overall acquiring a better understanding of privacy issues. BBC suggests that "as privacy settings become more sophisticated and awareness of how to use them increases, along with understanding of the potential consequences of leaving content in a public space, the more the availability of the content may be considered a matter of the user's responsibility" (2015a). This does not give BBC journalists a *carte blanche* to claim an "it's in the public domain" position. It does acknowledge that the attitudes and abilities around privacy are changing. However, this trend may not necessarily continue in the anticipated direction of an ever more relaxed attitude by younger generations. Present habits of social media use, especially in the younger generation, are shifting from open-network to closed-network applications, such as Snapchat and WhatsApp. The golden age of social media mining by journalists may have already reached its high point.

References

BBC. (2015a). *Editorial guidelines*. Accessed May 3, 2016 from http://www.bbc.co.uk/editorialguidelines/guidelines

BBC. (2015b). *Editorial guidelines*. Accessed May 3, 2016 from http://www.bbc.co.uk/editorialguidelines/guidance

Broersma, M., & Graham, T. (2013). Twitter as a new source. *Journalism Practice, 7*, 446–464. doi:10.1080/17512786.2013.802481.

Broersma, M., Den Herder, B., & Schohaus, B. (2013). A question of power. *Journalism Practice, 7*, 388–395. doi:10.1080/17512786.2013.802474.

Council of Europe. (1950). Convention for the protection of human rights and fundamental freedoms. In *European Convention on Human Rights, as Amended*. Strasbourg cedex: ECHR.

Curran, J. (1991). Rethinking the media as a public sphere. In P. Dahlgren & C. Sparks (Eds.), *Communication and citizenship* (pp. 267–284). London: Routledge.

Editors' Code of Practice Committee. (2015). *Editors' code of practice*. IPSO. Accessed November 20, 2015 from https://www.ipso.co.uk/IPSO/cop.html; Note: The 2015 Code is no longer available.

Editors' Code of Practice Committee. (2016). *Editors' code of practice*. IPSO. Accessed May 3, 2016 from https://www.ipso.co.uk/IPSO/cop.html

European Commission. (2015). *Special Eurobarometer 431: Data protection*. Brussels: European Commission: Directorate-General for Communication.

Gans, H. (1979). *Deciding what's news: A study of CBS evening news, NBC nightly news, Newsweek and Time*. New York: Vintage.

Greenslade, R. (2015). *Editors' code revised to prevent gender bias and wayward headlines*. Guardian.co.uk. Accessed May 2, 2016 from http://www.theguardian.com/media/greenslade/2015/dec/03/editors-code-revised-to-prevent-gender-bias-and-wayward-headlines

Hermida, A., Lewis, S. C., & Zamith, R. (2014). Sourcing the Arab spring: A case study of Andy Carvin's sources on twitter during the Tunisian and Egyptian revolutions. *Journal of Computer-Mediated Communication, 19*, 479–499.

HM Government. (1998). *Human rights act*. London: HMSO.

IPSO. (2015a). *04459–15 Rainford v Mirror.co.uk. IPSO*. Accessed May 3, 2016 from https://www.ipso.co.uk/IPSO/rulings/IPSOrulings-detail.html?id=231

IPSO. (2015b). *04426–15 Johnson v Dartmouth Chronicle*. IPSO. Accessed May 3, 2016 from https://www.ipso.co.uk/IPSO/rulings/IPSOrulings-detail.html?id=235

Jarvis, J. (2010). *Confusing *a* Public with *the* Public*. Accessed May 3, 2016 from http://buzzmachine.com/2010/05/08/confusing-a-public-with-the-public

O'Neill, K. (2015). *See 'giant rat' spotted at Burger King drive-thru as disgusted customer demands money back*. mirror.co.uk. Accessed May 3, 2016 from http://www.mirror.co.uk/news/uk-news/see-giant-rat-spotted-burger-5972812

Ofcom. (2015). *Broadcasting Code*. Ofcom. Accessed May 3, 2016 from http://stakeholders.ofcom.org.uk/broadcasting/broadcast-codes/broadcast-code/

Swigger, N. (2013). The online citizen: Is social media changing citizens' beliefs about democratic values? *Political Behavior, 35*, 589–603.

Watson, J., Lipford, H. R., & Besmer, A. (2015). Mapping user preference to privacy default settings. *ACM Transactions on Computer-Human Interaction, 22*, 1–20.

Part II
Discourses on Cybersecurity and Data Protection in Comparative Perspective

Analysing the French Discourse About "Surveillance and Data Protection" in the Context of the NSA Scandal

Methodological Reflections and Results in Terms of Content

Verena Weiland

1 Introduction

The revelations of the secret actions of the American National Security Agency (NSA) by Edward Snowden in June 2013 provoked a large political and public outcry in Europe. They served as a reason to discuss not only relations between the United States and the European Union in general, but also the concept of data protection and the legality of keeping people from other nations under surveillance. In France, different politicians commented on the secret information that Snowden made public all over the world, some of them searching for measures to stabilize the political situation and appease the public's displeasure. In the construction of such public discourses, the mass media play a fundamental role as they inform the public of this important event and of reactions to it. In fact, the revelations of the secret NSA actions began in June 2013, when *The Guardian* and *The Washington Post* started publishing internal documents that Edward Snowden had transmitted to them. This set off an enormous, intense and diverse discursive production in the media. For example, when we compare the number of articles containing the terms *NSA* or *National Security Agency* in French newspapers by the aid of the internet database *Nexis*,[1] we get 2030 articles published between June and August 2013, but only 53 articles published in the three months before. According to Sophie Moirand (2014), who tries to outline a definition of the French term *événement* (*event*) using the common dictionary *Le Petit Robert* 2012, an event is something that takes place

---

[1]The analysis includes "All Publications—France", the query is "[NSA] or [National Security Agency]". The first search covers the period between 01.06.2013 and 31.08.2013, the second the three months before that, thus 01.03.2013 until 31.05.2013.

V. Weiland (✉)
Universität Heidelberg, Romanisches Seminar, Seminarstr. 3, 69117 Heidelberg, Germany
e-mail: verena.weiland@rose.uni-heidelberg.de

© Springer International Publishing AG 2017
W.J. Schünemann, M.-O. Baumann (eds.), *Privacy, Data Protection and Cybersecurity in Europe*, DOI 10.1007/978-3-319-53634-7_4

or occurs[2] and that is of importance for human beings. Thus, it is also characterised by a social aspect. As some examples for terms that categorise events, Moirand lists *catastrophe (catastrophe)*, *désastre (disaster)*, *tragédie (tragedy)*, *drame (drama)* or *affaire (scandal/affair)*. Moreover, the term *événement (event)* is often combined with characterizations, i.e. *événement naturel/social/politique/historique (natural/ social/political/historical event)* or *événement médiatique (media event)*. Laura Calabrese explains how an event is related to the reporting on it and what role is attributed to language:

> When the press decides to create a discourse of an event, they either have to give it a name, take the representations which are already circulating or reformulate them. All of these operations produce a certain image of the event, of the actors and the conflicts between them; to some extent, the words which are chosen to speak of it include these conflicts, as well as the facts making up the event and the discourses that have been produced with regard to it [transl. by the author].[3]

As Calabrese outlines in the quotation, different aspects and conflicts in the context of an event find expression in the discourse. These facts will be the focus of the analysis presented in this chapter. In a first step, the designation of the event—in particular the use of the terms *révélation (revelation)* and *scandale (scandal)*—will be examined in order to point out the specific characteristics of the French perception of the NSA affair and the reactions to it. In a second step, different actors and conflicts linked to the understanding of surveillance and data protection will be pointed out. Finally, a special focus will be put on the various facets of the discourse that were shaped by discourse actors in France and the USA.

2   Analysing the *Revelations* as a Discursive Event

The corpus, which was built for this analysis, consists of French newspaper articles (both print articles and those from online platforms) and contains 32,860,355 tokens.[4] In each article at least one of the following lemmas[5] occurs: *sécurité, surveillance/surveiller*, or *contrôle/contrôler (security, surveillance/to keep under*

---

[2]"Ce qui arrive, c'est ce qui a lieu, ce qui se produit, ce qui survient [...]" (Moirand 2014).

[3]Orig. citation: "Lorsque la presse décide de mettre en discours un événement, elle doit soit le nommer, soit reprendre des désignations circulantes, soit les reformuler. Toutes ces opérations mettent en scène une certaine image de l'événement, de ses acteurs et des conflits qui les opposent; dans une certaine mesure, les mots choisis pour en rendre compte contiennent ces conflits, les faits qui constituent l'événement et les discours qui ont été produits par rapport à lui" (Calabrese 2006: 2).

[4]Census by Sketch Engine.

[5]A lemma is the form of a term that is used as an entry in the dictionary whereas a lexeme is the set of all forms that have the same meaning. A lemma thus is a representative of a lexeme (cf. Glück 2005: 376).

Table 1 Distributional thesaurus for the lemma *scandale*

Table	Score	Freq.
crise (crisis)	0.156	6102
polémique (polemic)	0.154	990
révélation (revelation)	0.152	2252
catastrophe (catastrophe)	0.149	1452
incident (incident)	0.139	2744
drame (drama)	0.137	2493
orage (storm)	0.129	1321
conflit (conflict)	0.126	2555
événement (event)	0.122	4790
tension (tension)	0.119	2690
affaire (affair)	0.117	16,857
panique (panic)	0.117	371
crime (crime)	0.117	1692
accusation (accusation)	0.116	1459

On the left side are the lemmas similar to the lemma *scandal*. Their similarity is ordered by a score that considers the grammatical and collocational distribution [For the score's calculation, see the Statistics used in Sketch Engine (2014): www.sketchengine.co.uk/documentation/raw-attachment/wiki/SkE/DocsIndex/ske-stat.pdf]. Freq. indicates the absolute frequency of the terms in the corpus

surveillance, control/to control.[6] Sophie Moirand lists some typical nouns and characterizing adjectives used to denote events that could also be of interest for the analysis. In order to analyse, for example, the lemma *scandale* (*scandal*), which seems to be the most appropriate term in Moirand's list (see above) for what happened in 2013 as a result of Snowden's actions, the so called distributional thesaurus is useful. It "consists of a ranked list of the lemmas most similar to the lemma entered in terms of grammatical and collocational behaviour"[7] but should not be confused with the analysis of semantic similarities found in a normal thesaurus entry. The following list (Table 1) shows the distributional thesaurus for the lemma *scandale* (*scandal*).

The occurrences of these lemmas show that there are different terms such as *crise* (*crisis*), *catastrophe* (*catastrophe*), *drame* (*drama*), *orage* (*storm*), *conflit* (*conflict*), *tension* (*tension*), *panique* (*panic*), *crime* (*crime*) or *accusation* (*accusation*) with very expressive meanings and negative connotations. Nevertheless, it is important not only to analyse these isolated terms but to put them into contexts in order to confirm that they really refer to Snowden's actions and to see if they are used differently from each other. The function Word Sketch reveals, for example,

---

[6]The exact query is: [sécurité! OR surveill! OR contrôle!], so that composed and plural forms can be found at the basis of the lexemes. 82 sources in Nexis are taken into consideration. The selection criteria are: (i) news in French language, (ii) published in France, (iii) web based publications and newspaper articles, (iv) no identic duplicates.

[7]Thesaurus Entry, Sketch Engine (2015), https://www.sketchengine.co.uk/thesaurus-entry/

that the term *scandale* (*scandale*) does not only appear together with the adjectives *politique* (*political*) or *international* (*international*), but also with *planétaire* (*planetary*) or *alimentaire* (*food*), thus not exclusively referring to the NSA. The lemma *crise* (*crisis*) collocates, on the one hand, with the adjectives *économique* (*economic*, 413x), *politique* (*political*, 300x), *transatlantique* (*transatlantic*, 10x) or *sé curitaire* (*security*, 9x), and on the other hand, it can also be found together with *syrien* (*Syrian*, 146x), *financier* (*financial*, 214x), *bancaire* (*bank*, 52x) or *humanitaire* (*humanitarian*, 21x). However, as the focus in this chapter is not a linguistic one, these two examples should be sufficient to show the variety of collocations that can be found in the corpus. In the following, the focus will be on the collocations in the context of Edward Snowden and the NSA so that the main characteristics will become apparent.

At first, the analysis of the noun *scandale* reveals interesting aspects; most frequently, it appears as an object of the verb *révélér* (*to reveal*). This raises the question of who the actors revealing the scandals are and which scandals are mentioned in the corpus. Regarding the collocations *scandale de/du + noun* (*scandale of + noun*), Word Sketch lists the *corruption scandal* (*corruption*, 51x), the *bugging scandal* (*écoute*, 32x), the *espionage scandal* (*espionnage*, 26x), the *manipulation scandal* (*manipulation*, 11x), and the *surveillance scandal* (*surveillance*, 9x).[8] In addition, there is the scandal of a *programme* (*programme*, 16x) that has to be analysed more precisely to understand its importance for the French discourse. In fact, it refers to the secret American programme PRISM, mentioned in the following examples: "le scandale des programmes américains de cybersurveillance et d'écoutes" (*Le Figaro Newsflash*, 01.07.2013), "le scandale du vaste programme secret de surveillance de la NSA" (*Sud Ouest*, 28.08.2013) or "le scandale du vaste programme d'écoutes et de collecte d'informations de la NSA" (*France 24*, 18.06.2013).[9] In the next step, analysis will show who the actors in the scandal are by having a closer look at the subjects of the verb *révéler* (*to reveal*). Here, we find the following three main actors:

1. The *New York Times*, ex.: "[...] the New York Times reveals a vast and illegal scandal of surveillance [...]" [transl. by the author], in *Le Monde*, 10.08.2013,[10]
2. The British daily *The Guardian*, ex.: "The British daily contributed to the revelation of the PRISM scandal [...]" [transl. by the author], in *Le Monde*, 24.08.2013,[11]

---

[8] Additionally, we find the *doping scandal* (*dopage*, 14x), the *lasagne scandal* (*lasagne*, 8x) and the *milk scandal* (*lait*, 6x) that, from a semantic point of view, don't have any relevance for the analysis of the NSA affair.

[9] *The scandal of the American cybersurveillance and bugging programme* (*Le Figaro Newsflash*, 01.07.2013), *the scandal of the NSA's vast secret programme of surveillance* (*Sud Ouest*, 28.08.2013), *the scandal of the NSA's vast programme bugging and collecting information* (*France 24*, 18.06.2013; translation by the author).

[10] Orig. citation: "[...] le New York Times révèle un vaste scandale de surveillance illégale [...]".

[11] Orig. citation: "Le quotidien britannique a contribué à révéler le scandale Prism [...]".

3. Edward Snowden, ex.: "[. . .] this young computer specialist, working for a service provider of the NSA, who revealed the scandal of the system PRISM [. . .]" [transl. by the author], in *Le Figaro*, 10.06.2013.[12]

Another important aspect is the range of the scandal in respect to the states and the persons involved. Regarding the adjectives that characterise the lemma *scandale* (*scandal*), the collocation *scandale mondial* (*worldwide scandal*) can be found several times. The internet portal of *Le Parisien*, for example, even provides a chronology of the revelations titled *L'affaire Snowden, un scandale mondial* (*The Snowden affair, a worldwide scandal*, i.e. mentioned in *Le Parisien.fr*, 10.08.2013). One approach to gathering information about the character of an event, the people involved and the subsequent consequences, is the analysis of co-occurrences of terms that mark events. For example, when looking at the verbs *déclencher* (*to set off*) and *prolonger* (*to prolong/to stretch out*), we quickly find out that Edward Snowden was the one to reveal the scandal, that it involves the subject of surveillance and that it concerns not only enterprises, but also French and European private citizens. Furthermore, new questions about the involvement of other actors arise. The following example shows, nevertheless, that it is important to consider different denominations as well. Here, the noun *affaire* (*affair*) replaces *scandale* (*scandal*):

> The scandal that was set off by the affair of Snowden and the revelation of the surveillance exerted on citizens, enterprises, etc., by the American National Security Agency (NSA), continues the complicity between Western secret services, notably the German and the American. This affair has given rise to more protests and reactions in Germany than in France [transl. by the author] (*Le Monde.fr*, 12.08.2013).[13]

As we come to know in the last sentence, the NSA scandal provoked stronger reactions in Germany than in France—a fact that will also be of importance for the analysis of the discourse actors. However, since it is not possible to analyse each of the lemmas listed at the beginning of this subsection in this essay, only the most interesting and expedient aspects will be mentioned. The lemma *crise*, for example, is one of the lemmas that refer to very different domains. Nevertheless, two main aspects should be highlighted: the espionage affair is seen in many cases as a "political crisis" (*crise politique*) between the US and the European Union,[14] and it is also described as a "transatlantic crisis" (*crise transatlantique*). This excerpt

---

[12]Orig. citation: "[. . .] ce jeune informaticien, employé par un prestataire de services de la NSA, qui a révélé le scandale du système PRISM [. . .]".

[13]Orig. citation: "Le scandale déclenché par l'affaire Snowden et la révélation de la surveillance exercée sur les citoyens, les entreprises, etc., par l'Agence nationale de sécurité américaine (NSA), se prolonge par celui de la complicité entre services de renseignement occidentaux, notamment allemands, et américains".

[14]Ex.: "L'espionnage par les États-Unis crée une crise politique avec l'Europe" (*Les Echos.fr*, 09.03.2016)/"The espionage by the United States creates a political crisis with Europe" [translation by the author].

from an article in the daily *Le Monde* even draws a comparison to the Iraq War:
"[...] the affair Edward Snowden, a former employee of the NSA, whose recent
revelations have set off a crisis in transatlantic relations unprecedented since the
intervention in Iraq" [transl. by the author] (*Le Monde*, 03.07.2013).[15]

One of the most expressive lemmas is *révélation* (*revelation*), with a total
frequency of 2252 in the corpus including 99 instances of the co-occurrence *révé
lations fracassantes* ("sensational revelations") and 24 instances of the
co-occurrence *révélations explosifs* ("explosive revelations"). All in all, the analysis of this lemma reveals a strong emotional aspect, as we can also see in the two
following examples concerning the reactions of different political authorities to the
revelations: "These revelations have set off a strong agitation in Brussels" [transl.
by the author] (*Le Point.fr*, 10.08.2013)[16] or "The revelations set off the scepticism
of the principal European powers" [transl. by the author] (*Le Parisien*,
20.08.2013).[17] These citations show the worldwide indignation and indicate that
the revelations provoked political consequences in Europe. The French media also
gave particular attention to the reactions in Germany: "These revelations provoked
a lot of criticism within the political scene in Germany, especially within the
opposition" [transl. by the author] (*France 24*, 05.08.2013).[18] Furthermore, when
having a look at those who are responsible for the revelations, another actor can be
found apart from Edward Snowden, *The New York Times* and *The Guardian* that
were already mentioned above: the German weekly *Der Spiegel* played a major
role. In fact, the collocation *révélations du Spiegel* ("revelations of *Der Spiegel*")
appears 25 times in the corpus, each one on 1 July 2013, after *Der Spiegel* had just
published some new details about the surveillance strategies of the NSA:

> According to *Der Spiegel*, the programme did not only consist of installed micros in the
> buildings of the EU in Washington, but also of an infiltration of the computer network
> which made it possible to read the electronic mail and internal documents. The represen-
> tation of the EU in the UNO was under surveillance in the same way and according to these
> documents, the Europeans are explicitly designated as 'targets to attack' [transl. by the
> author] (*Centre Presse*, 01.07.2013).[19]

---

[15]Orig. citation: "[...] l'affaire Edward Snowden, l'ancien employé de la NSA dont les dernières
révélations ont entraîné une crise dans les relations transatlantiques sans précédent depuis
l'intervention en Irak".

[16]Orig. citation: "Ces révélations avaient suscité un grand émoi à Bruxelles".

[17]Orig. citation: "Ces révélations ont suscité le scepticisme des principales puissances
européennes".

[18]Orig. citation: "Ces révélations suscitent de vives critiques au sein de la scène politique
allemande et notamment de l'opposition".

[19]Orig. citation: "Selon Der Spiegel, le programme était constitué non seulement de micros
installés dans le bâtiment de l'UE à Washington, mais aussi d'une infiltration du réseau
informatique qui lui permettait de lire les courriers électroniques et les documents internes. La
représentation de l'UE à l'ONU était surveillée de la même manière, toujours selon ces documents,
dans lesquels les Européens sont explicitement désignés comme des 'cibles à attaquer' ".

On the basis of this information, it is important to note that the Germans seem to play an important role in the French discourse which will be analysed in detail in the following subsection.

3   Political Discourse Actors: *Friends, Allies* and *Partners*

The Word List function can be helpful in researching the political actors leaving their mark on the French media discourse. After all lemmas that refer to nations are selected, i.e. *américain (American), français (French), allemand (German), États-Unis (US)*, etc., the Word Sketch helps bring them into contexts. Furthermore, qualitative analysis should also be done and seen as a complementary approach to the quantitative analysis. As a result, it appears that many of the texts, although they refer to the subject of security and surveillance, do not concern the NSA. Some of them focus on Turkey, for example, especially the Turkish Prime Minister. However, these articles mostly concern the security during protests against the Turkish government in Istanbul in 2013.[20] Furthermore, Great Britain, China and Russia are also linked to the subject of surveillance and security in the French discourse. The connection to China and Russia is a more pragmatic one, as it concerns the information about Edward Snowden's escape: "[...] Edward Snowden, who worked for a subcontractor of the American agency, fled from Hong Kong (China) to Russia in the hope of getting to another country" [transl. by the author] (*Le Monde.fr*, 01.08.2013).[21]

The lemma *allemand* occurs with different political expressions that, when adding some qualitative analysis, can be confirmed to be referring to the NSA. The nouns concerned are[22]: *chancelière (chancellor*, 119x), *ministre (minister*, 81x), *gouvernement (government*, 87x), *économie (economy*, 41x), *justice (justice*, 27x). Besides these expressions, the lemmas *magazine (magazine), hebdomadaire (weekly*, 22x), *presse (press*, 28x) as well as *renseignement (information*, 26x) appear in the list. *Renseignement* is part of the collocation *service de renseignement (intelligence agency)* in 25 of 26 cases. In fact, the more far-reaching qualitative analysis of each of these lemmas clearly show that Germany plays a fundamental role in the French discourse on security and surveillance. At the centre of attention are the revelations of the weekly *Der Spiegel* and the German reaction to the NSA scandal, exemplified in the following quote:

---

[20]Apart from Turkey, Spain, Egypt, Mali and other nations are also itemized. However, they don't refer to the context of interest, so that they will not be taken into consideration hereafter.

[21]Orig. citation: "Edward Snowden, qui travaillait pour un sous-traitant de l'agence américaine, s'est envolé depuis Hongkong (Chine) vers la Russie, dans l'espoir de rejoindre un autre pays".

[22]Sorted by salience according to Sketch Engine (2016), see https://www.sketchengine.co.uk/word-sketch/.

The revelations concerning the involvement of the German Federal Intelligence Service (BND) in the web espionage programme led by the American National Security Agency (NSA) provoked a real storm across the Rhine [transl. by the author] (*Le Point.fr*, 17.07.2013).[23]

However, articles about the indignation in Germany principally seem to compare the reactions to those in France and to point out that Germany, not France, is the main target of the NSA:

And the latest revelations of *Der Spiegel*, published yesterday afternoon, risk to set the German opinion on fire, which is very sensitive about questions concerning the protection of private life. In fact, Germany is 'the European country kept under the most surveillance' by the NSA, with 500 million telephone and internet connections registered per month, assures the magazine, explaining that a 'normal' day of espionage is about 15 million phone calls recorded in Germany, against about two million per day in France [transl. by the author] (*Charente Libre*, 01.07.2013).[24]

In a press release, the White House reported that 'the President had assured the chancellor [Angela Merkel] that the United States takes the anxiety of our European allies and partners seriously' [transl. by the author] (*Les Echos.fr*, 04.07.2013).[25]

Thus, the French reaction to the NSA has several characteristics: the first one is that the new information in the German *Spiegel* is of great importance for the French discourse, since the French press cannot provide any new information, leaving them dependent on the German and British media. In addition, detailed information on reactions of individual German politicians are given, often including citations. It is important to note that the comparison to the Cold War plays a fundamental role as illustrated in the following extract:

The German Minister of Justice, Sabine Leutheusser-Schnarrenberger, appeared to be scathing: 'It is beyond comprehension that our American friends consider the Europeans as enemies [...] This is reminiscent of actions between enemies during the Cold War' [transl. by the author] (*L'Est Républicain*, 01.07.2013).[26]

---

[23]Orig. citation: "Les révélations concernant l'implication du Service fédéral de renseignements allemand (BND) dans le programme d'espionnage du Web mené par l'Agence nationale de sécurité américaine (NSA) ont provoqué une véritable tempête outre-Rhin".

[24]Orig. citation: "Et les toutes dernières révélations du Spiegel, faites hier après-midi, risquent d'enflammer l'opinion allemande, très sensible sur les questions de protection de la vie privée. L'Allemagne est en effet 'le pays européen le plus surveillé' par la NSA, avec 500 millions de connexions téléphoniques et Internet enregistrées mensuellement, assure le magazine, qui explique qu'une journée 'normale' d'espionnage y tourne autour de 15 millions d'appels téléphoniques recensés en Allemagne, pour environ deux millions quotidiennement en France".

[25]Orig. citation: "Dans un communiqué, la Maison blanche a rapporté que 'le président avait assuré à la chancelière [Angela Merkel] que les Etats-Unis prennent au sérieux les inquiétudes de nos alliés et partenaires européens'".

[26]Orig. citation: "La ministre allemande de la Justice, Sabine Leutheusser-Schnarrenberger, s'est montrée cinglante : 'Cela dépasse l'entendement que nos amis américains considèrent les Européens comme des ennemis [...] Ce n'est pas sans rappeler des actions entre ennemis pendant la Guerre froide'."

In total, the collocation *Guerre Froide* occurs 337 times in the corpus and it is conspicuous that the French media frequently emphasize that the Germans were the first to draw this comparison:

> NSA/US: Berlin is bringing up the Cold War [...] A little bit earlier, Germany had estimated that the US displayed 'unacceptable' behaviour worthy of the Cold War if it should prove to be true that the National Security Agency (NSA) had led a large programme bugging the European Union (EU) [transl. by the author] (*Le Figaro Newsflash*, 01.07.2013).[27]

Another important characteristic of the discourse is that the relations between the European states and the US are fought out in a linguistic way. This is especially done by weighing up the semantic differences between the expressions *ami* (*friend*), *allié* (*ally*) and *partenaire* (*partner*) as in the quote of Sabine Leutheusser-Schnarrenberger cited above. The German Minister of Justice emphasizes that the Americans are seen as friends by the European states and assumes that on the part of the US it is the other way around as they consider Europe their "enemies" (*L'Est Républicain*, 01.07.2013). Germany and France agree that the American espionage is not compatible with the concepts of *friendship* and *partnership* between states. Furthermore, the French politicians do not seem to be sure how to speak about the United States, that is to say, about whether to consider them *friends*—surely the expression for a close international relationship between states—or as *allies* or *partners*, two expressions that accentuate cooperation between states with the aim to reach common political or economic objectives. The following examples illustrate that while the French and German politicians adhere to the expressions *ami*, *allié* and *partenaire* for designating the US, they also make it clear that their confidence has been shaken and that espionage will not be tolerated:

> 'The espionage of friends is unacceptable', warned Steffen Siebert [sic!], spokesperson of Chancellor Angela Merkel. 'The confidence has to be re-established,' he added [translation by the author] (*Le Populaire du Centre*, 02.07.2013).[28]

> Michel Barnier, the French Commissioner, also reacted on his Twitter account, declaring that 'clarity, truth and transparency are what we can and should expect from our friends and allies' [translation by the author] (*Le Figaro Online*, 1.07.2013).[29]

Nevertheless, against the backdrop of the high importance of the international relations between the European Union and the US, the French President cannot

---

[27]Orig. citation: "NSA/US : Berlin évoque la guerre froide [...] Un peu plus tôt, l'Allemagne avait estimé que les Etats-Unis auraient un comportement 'inacceptable' et digne de la guerre froide, s'il était avéré que l'Agence nationale de sécurité (NSA) avait mené un vaste programme d'écoute de l'Union européenne (UE)."

[28]Orig. citation: " 'L'espionnage d'amis est inacceptable', a averti Steffen Siebert [sic!], porte-parole de la chancelière Angela Merkel. 'La confiance doit être rétablie', a-t-il ajouté."

[29]Orig. citation: "Michel Barnier, le commissaire français, a également réagi sur son compte Twitter en déclarant que 'clarté, vérité et transparence sont ce que l'on peut et doit attendre de nos amis et alliés'."

announce concrete actions against the American surveillance but can only invoke morality:

> 'We can't accept this type of behaviour between partners and allies', declared M. Hollande during a visit in Lorient. 'We demand for this to be stopped immediately', he added [. . .] [transl. by the author] (*Le Figaro Newsflash*, 1.07.2016).[30]

In contrast, it should be mentioned that the French government's faith in the US obviously had not been shaken too seriously, as at the end of August, approximately three months after the NSA scandal had become public and in the context of the war in Syria, the French government declared that the US were "close friends":

> If Barack Obama brings up a limited military action in Syria, at present, France seems the best partner for such an engagement. After a discussion with Barack Obama on the telephone, the *Elysée* speaks of 'close allies and friends' [transl. by the author] (*RFI* [*Radio France Internationale*], 31.08.2013).[31]

4 Analysing a Specific Term: *Protection des données/Data Protection*

Another consequence of the revelations by Edward Snowden is the discussion about how to improve data protection. In the French discourse, the media warn about the fact that not only companies, but also most regular citizens[32] are affected by the American surveillance as the NSA, according to Edward Snowden, obligates the American giant firms Google, Facebook and Microsoft to transfer collected data to them:

> Last week, these new revelations forced, for example, American Amazon to gather one thousand French companies whose data they store, in order to try, with difficulty, to reassure them about the security of the information that had been entrusted to them. These new developments will not reassure the general public which is already increasingly worried about the precariousness of the data protection and the protection of private life in the digital universe [transl. by the author] (*Sud Ouest*, 01.07.2013).[33]

---

[30]Orig. citation: "'Nous ne pouvons pas accepter ce type de comportement entre partenaires et alliés', a déclaré M. Hollande en marge d'une visite à Lorient. 'Nous demandons que cela cesse immédiatement', a-t-il ajouté [. . .]".

[31]Orig. citation: "Si Barack Obama évoque une action militaire limitée en Syrie, la France paraît actuellement le meilleur partenaire pour un tel engagement. L'Elysée parle de 'proches alliés et amis' après un entretien au téléphone avec Barack Obama."

[32]According to an article published in *Sud Ouest* on the 01.07.2013, there are about 42 million French accounts on Facebook, Twitter and Google.

[33]Orig. citation: "Ces révélations ont par exemple contraint l'américain Amazon à réunir la semaine dernière un millier d'entreprises françaises dont il héberge les données informatiques pour, péniblement, tenter de les rassurer sur la sécurisation des informations qui lui sont confiées. Ces nouveaux rebondissements ne vont pas rassurer le grand public, déjà de plus en plus inquiet quant à la précarité de la protection des données et de la vie privée dans l'univers numérique."

The revelations by Edward Snowden seem to have risen public awareness of the need for better data protection and the improvement of the law on free access to administrative documents and the freedom of information adopted in 1978.[34] The European dimension is seen as being of great importance in two different ways for French data protection. Firstly, France depends on the European legal situation; secondly, some French politicians demand to attach demands for stopping the NSA surveillance to negotiations of the free trade agreement with the United States:

> Moreover, the German Chancellor, Angela Merkel, the French President, François Hollande, and the President of the European Commission, José Manuel Barroso, wanted to take advantage of their participation in the conference on the employment of young people in Europe [. . .] on Wednesday in order to present a common answer to Washington. The negotiations about the free trade agreement will not start 'without opening a discussion and a verification with the United States about their secret service activities in our countries and about the protection of private data at the same time', declared M. Hollande [. . .] [transl. by the author] (*Le Monde*, 05.07.2013).[35]

> 'Between partners one does not spy!' said Viviane Reding, European Commissioner of Justice, in Luxembourg yesterday. 'We cannot negotiate about a great transatlantic market if there is the faintest doubt that our partners are attempting to bug the offices of the European negotiator', she warned [. . .] [transl. by the author] (*Centre Presse*, 1.07.2013).[36]

The speakers in the French debate mostly agree that a solution to the data protection problem cannot be found within France, but rather needs to be Europe-wide.[37] In

---

[34]*Loi n° 78-17 du 6 janvier* (1978) *relative à l'informatique, aux fichiers et aux libertés*, https://www.cnil.fr/fr/loi-78-17-du-6-janvier-1978-modifiee

[35]Orig. citation: "La chancelière allemande, Angela Merkel, le président français, François Hollande, et celui de la Commission européenne, José Manuel Barroso, ont par ailleurs souhaité profiter de leur participation, mercredi, à la conférence [. . .] sur l'emploi des jeunes en Europe pour présenter une réponse commune à Washington. Les négociations sur le traité de libre-échange ne démarreront pas 'sans qu'il y ait à la même date ouverture de discussions et de vérifications avec les Etats-Unis sur les activités des services de renseignements américains dans nos pays et sur la protection des données privées', a déclaré M. Hollande [...]."

[36]Orig. citation: "'Entre partenaires, on n'espionne pas !', a lancé hier au Luxembourg la commissaire européenne à la Justice, Viviane Reding. 'On ne peut pas négocier sur un grand marché transatlantique s'il y a le moindre doute que nos partenaires ciblent des écoutes vers les bureaux des négociateurs européens', a-t-elle averti [. . .]".

[37]"Contrôle des données personnelles/En la matière, les gouvernements européens sont très divisés. Certains craignent que les entreprises soient trop pénalisées, d'autres veulent se concentrer sur les réseaux sociaux, ou alors jugent le projet trop flou. Certes, en 2010 et 2012, les Européens ont réussi à limiter l'accès des Américains au contrôle des flux financiers en Europe et aux données personnelles des passagers. Mais ils peinent à adopter une position commune face au risque d'intrusions américaines de plus en plus massives dans les échanges électroniques en Europe" (*RFI*, 11.07.2013)./"Control of personal data/Concerning this subject, the European governments are very divided. Some of them fear that the companies would be penalised too much, others want to concentrate on the social networks or judge the project as too vague. Certainly, in 2010 and 2012, the Europeans succeeded in limiting America's access to the control of financial fluxes in Europe and to personal data of passengers. But they struggle with adopting a common position in view of the risk of America's intrusion in the electronic exchanges increasingly massive in Europe" (translation by the author).

addition, they consent to the fact that protecting personal data on the internet is very difficult. Nevertheless, there are also articles giving security advice to citizens. Yet again, the French press cares about which appropriate measures are taken in Germany:

> This is why Deutsche Telekom and United Internet assure that the email transfers between their servers are also encrypted, so that they allow sending secure emails between the clients of the networks T-Online, web.de and gmx. Finally, the two companies announced that their users' emails were exclusively stored on servers based in Germany, so that concerning the protection of personal data they were subordinated to German law, one of the most sophisticated in the world. The initiative was greeted by smiles from the Chaos Computer Club, a famous German association of hackers [transl. by the author] (*Le Monde. fr*, 10.08.2013).[38]

Another interesting point of view is presented by Jean-Luc Mélenchon (left-wing party) and from the ecologist party, which formed part of the government of François Hollande and Jean-Marc Ayrault at the time. They sought political asylum for Edward Snowden in order to demonstrate vehemently against the American surveillance programme:

> According to the French ecologist party, granting political asylum to the computer scientist [...] is a way of reminding that Paris 'clearly refuses the American line on data protection and the obvious violations of the fundamental public liberties in the name of its fight against the terrorist risk' [transl. by the author] (*France 24*, 1.07.2013).[39]

As this citation shows, another aspect has to be considered when debating the subject of secret surveillance: the practical use of surveillance for security reasons.

5 Espionage Programmes in the Name of Security Measures?

For the French President Hollande, the argument of preventing terrorist attacks is important. However, we have to distinguish between the surveillance actions of the American NSA and those of the French intelligence service. Hollande avoids articulating any concerns about the latter but gives it a word of praise and accentuates its necessity:

---

[38]Orig. citation: "C'est pourquoi Deutsche Telekom et United Internet assurent que les transferts de mails entre leurs serveurs seront également cryptés, permettant un envoi de mails sécurisés entre tous les clients des réseaux T-Online, web.de et gmx. Enfin, les deux entreprises ont annoncé que les courriels de leurs utilisateurs seraient exclusivement conservés sur des serveurs basés en Allemagne, ce qui les place sous le régime du droit allemand en matière de protection des données personnelles, un des plus sophistiqués au monde. L'initiative fait sourire le groupe Chaos Computer Club, célèbre association allemande de hackers."

[39]Orig. citation: "Selon le parti écologiste français, accorder l'asile politique à l'informaticien [...] est une façon de rappeler que Paris 'refuse clairement le diktat américain sur la protection des données et les violations manifestes des libertés publiques fondamentales au nom de sa lutte contre le risque terroriste'."

'In the face of the increasing terrorist menace, the President of the Republic saluted the work of the intelligence services and thanked the national coordinator [. . .]', concluded the Elysée. The French Intelligence Service includes about 11,000 persons. The principal services are the general management of the exterior security service (DGSE), the central management of the interior security service, the management of the military security service (DRM) and the management of protection and defense security (DPSD) [transl. by the author] (*Les Echos.fr*, 10.06.2013).[40]

One could expect a detailed discussion about the actual French intelligence service, but no such discussion took place. Yet, it is interesting to see that the politicians in Europe and America each offer glimpses into their respective worldviews by talking about *espionage* or *security measures* when referring to the subject of surveillance. In some articles, the authors question whether the work of the NSA should be seen as a system to avoid terrorist attacks or to threaten the citizens' liberty and the privacy of their personal data. In the corpus that covers the period between 1 June and 31 August 2013, no statement from François Hollande or any other French politician justifying the work of the NSA can be found. However, the prevention of terrorist attacks is the main argument brought forward by the US, and there is an important statement by Barack Obama that reveals his strategy of convincing critics of the advantages and reliability of the American intelligence services and tries to persuade his audience of the American point of view:

I came in with a healthy skepticism about these programs. My team evaluated them. We scrubbed them thoroughly. We actually expanded some of the oversight, increased some of the safeguards. But my assessment and my team's assessment was that they help us prevent terrorist attacks. And the modest encroachments on the privacy that are involved in getting phone numbers or duration without a name attached and not looking at content, that on net, it was worth us doing. Some other folks may have a different assessment on that. But I think it's important to recognize that you can't have 100 percent security and also then have 100 percent privacy and zero inconvenience. We're going to have to make some choices as a society. [. . .] And in the abstract, you can complain about Big Brother and how this is a potential program run amok, but when you actually look at the details, then I think we've struck the right balance. (07.06.2013)[41]

The following day, *LeMonde.fr* published an article about Obama's speech without discussing the consequences of the NSA's surveillance for France. The subject seemed only to affect the American nation: "The debate about cybersecurity at the expense of spying on citizens, contrary to the individual liberty, causes a stir in the

---

[40]Orig. citation: " 'Face à la montée de la menace terroriste, le président de la République a salué l'action des services de renseignement et remercié le coordonnateur national [...]', conclut l'Elysée. La communauté française du renseignement compte près de 11.000 personnes. Les principaux services sont la Direction générale de la sécurité extérieure (DGSE), la Direction centrale du renseignement intérieur (DCRI), la Direction du renseignement militaire (DRM) et la Direction de la protection et de la sécurité de la défense (DPSD)."

[41]URL: https://www.whitehouse.gov/the-press-office/2013/06/07/statement-president   (03.02. 2016). The statement is part of the corpus, yet translated into French, i.e. in *Le Monde.fr*, 07.06.: *Pour Obama, il faut faire des "compromis" entre sécurité et vie privée/For Obama, we have to make "compromises" between security and private life.*

US" [transl. by the author] (*LeMonde.fr*, 08.06.2016).[42] Other articles focus on Obama's argumentation within the context of public security, on the illegal transfer of secret state documents and on the actors involved in the surveillance program PRISM. The consequences for France are in no way at the centre of interest.

6 Conclusion

To summarise the results of the analysis, it is important to emphasize that the revelations of Edward Snowden in June 2013 set off a large discourse in the French media. In the following three months, different subjects related to the secret actions of the NSA were discussed. Indignation was the first important reaction, as the NSA's work was seen as *espionage* and *surveillance* threatening not only France, but also European politics, its companies and citizens; it was also criticised as undermining the confidence between Europe and the US. For these reasons, the scandal is often connected to the negotiation of the transatlantic free trade agreement, as some politicians argue that espionage between *partners*, *allies* or *friends* could not be tolerated. All in all, the French press seems to report about the revelations and the consequences of the NSA scandal from a European perspective. Especially the German politicians play an important role, because France considers Germany to be the country most affected by the American surveillance. Besides that, the NSA's secret actions were principally revealed by the English press and by the German *Spiegel*, not, however, by the French press. Nevertheless, from the way that the French politicians adopted the European point of view concerning this subject, one could suspect that they wanted to keep the public's attention from their own national surveillance programs. The articles in the corpus only cover the three months after Edward Snowden's revelations. In order to give an account of the current positions of the French and other European politicians, further research needs to be done, e.g. by observing a longer period of time.

References

Calabrese, L. (2006). La construction de la mémoire historico-médiatique à travers les désignations d'événements. In *Studies van de BKL 2006 /Travaux du CBL 2006/Papers of the LSB 2006* (pp. 2–16). Accessed March 17, 2016, from http://uahost.uantwerpen.be/linguist/SBKL/paps2006/cal2006.pdf
Glück, H. (2005). Lemma. In H. Glück (Ed.), *Metzler Lexikon Sprache* (3rd ed., p. 376). Stuttgart/Weimar: Metzler.

---

[42]Orig. citation: "Le débat sur la cyber-sécurité, au prix d'un espionnage des citoyens contraire aux libertés individuelles, fait rage aux États-Unis."

Loi n° 78-17 du 6 janvier. (1978). relative à l'informatique, aux fichiers et aux libertés. Accessed March 17, 2016, from www.cnil.fr/fr/loi-78-17-du-6-janvier-1978-modifiee

Moirand, S. (2014). L'événement 'saisi' par la langue et la communication. In *Cahiers de praxé matique, 63*. Accessed March 17, 2016, from http://praxematique.revues.org/2362

Sketch Engine. (2014). *Statistics used in Sketch Engine*. Accessed March 17, 2016, from www.sketchengine.co.uk/documentation/raw-attachment/wiki/SkE/DocsIndex/ske-stat.pdf

Sketch Engine. (2015). *Thesaurus*. Accessed March 17, 2016, from www.sketchengine.co.uk/thesaurus-entry/

Sketch Engine. (2016). *Word Sketch*. Accessed March 17, 2016, from www.sketchengine.co.uk/word-sketch/

Solving the Surveillance Problem

Media Debates About Unwanted Surveillance in Finland

Minna Tiainen

1 Introduction

The Snowden revelations, starting in the summer of 2013 and exposing a multitude of pervasive surveillance practices conducted by the US National Security Agency (NSA) and its partners, were the biggest intelligence leaks in recent history (cf. e.g. Lyon 2015). Around the world, heated media discussion, political conflicts and demands for reform followed the revelations. These surveillance discussions and especially the demands for change that were presented in them are the concern of the present article.

The rapid development and spread of digital technology have made surveillance unprecedentedly pervasive in recent decades (e.g. Mathiesen 2012: xix), but it took the Snowden leaks to make the issue the kind of global concern it is today (Lyon 2015: 13). The revelations can thus be seen as a key moment in the (global) societal awareness of surveillance. Understandably, the ensuing public discussion has become a site of struggle over the legitimacy of surveillance (e.g. Schulze 2015), that is, a place where vehement criticism meets staunch defence. Although such discussions take place on various societal platforms, the media can be considered a prime site for the struggle (see below). As part of the debate, alternatives and improvements to the current situation are sought, and change is demanded. In other words, the media discussion is also an important platform where solutions to the problem of surveillance are negotiated. This article aims to shed light on precisely this aspect of the media debate. It examines how solutions to the surveillance problem are constructed and debated in Finnish media coverage of the Snowden revelations and explores their contribution to the overall struggle over the legitimacy and future of surveillance.

M. Tiainen (✉)
Department of Language and Communication Studies, University of Jyväskylä, Jyväskylä, Finland
e-mail: minna.k.tiainen@jyu.fi

© Springer International Publishing AG 2017
W.J. Schünemann, M.-O. Baumann (eds.), *Privacy, Data Protection and Cybersecurity in Europe*, DOI 10.1007/978-3-319-53634-7_5

To make sense of these debates, this article draws on insights from both surveillance studies and Critical Discourse Studies (CDS). It adopts the view from surveillance studies of the societal relevance of surveillance. Following, among others, Fuchs (2008) and Lyon (2015), I understand surveillance to have central societal power, including the potential to threaten some core democratic principles and essential civil rights such as privacy (also cf. Foucault 1977). Snowden's extensive surveillance revelations underline the relevance of these concerns. From CDS, the article leans on the understanding that meaning is discursively constructed in language and other semiotic modes, from which emanates the societal significance of media discussions. I begin with the assumption that language use both shapes and is shaped by social factors and thus, for its part, contributes to the way societal power relations are organized (e.g. Wodak and Meyer 2016b; Pietikäinen and Mäntynen 2009; Foucault 1972). Established ways of discussing a particular matter constrain what can be said, imagined and considered possible (cf. e.g. Fairclough 1995: 56; Foucault 1972 for *discourses*), which means that the ways the surveillance debates construct possible resolutions of the situation are highly relevant for the future of surveillance.

As part of a more comprehensive research project that examines Finnish surveillance discussions post-Snowden, this article analyses media debates in Finland's leading newspaper, *Helsingin Sanomat*. Finland offers a rich site for the exploration of surveillance since it is a country that, on the one hand, prides itself on its technological sophistication and great respect for civil rights and, on the other hand, has outdated intelligence legislation which it plans to change in order to grant intelligence-gathering authorities a significantly broader mandate for surveillance. Additionally, the Finnish media are interesting since, as a platform for public discourse, they form the nexus of political, legal, technical and other relevant discussions about surveillance. The media play an essential role in bringing together key national and global actors and challenging (some of) them to take part in the surveillance discussion, which is particularly important considering the global nature of both the problems and possible solutions (as will become evident later; cf. Lyon 2015). I have chosen to analyse *Helsingin Sanomat* since it is the most respected Finnish daily newspaper and the only one claiming national reach. Its unique position in the Finnish media landscape guarantees that its "views and editorial decisions are often echoed in other media" (Kumpu 2016: 146).

In the next section, I will elaborate on my understanding of surveillance and discourse studies. After this, I will discuss the data and methodology before turning to the analysis of the different kinds of solutions in section "Overview of Solutions in the Surveillance Debate". Section "Conclusion" concludes with a discussion of the findings.

2 Theoretical Background: Surveillance and Media Discourse

2.1 Surveillance

Following Lyon (2015: 3), I understand surveillance basically as "collecting information in order to manage or control". It can be conducted by many kinds of actors, predominantly states and private companies. NSA and other state-conducted surveillance is, thus, only one example of current surveillance, yet a particularly interesting one since the revelations "reflect [the] resort to surveillance in many contexts" (ibid.: vii) and, above all, exemplify the major and probably most invasive trends in surveillance today (c.f. ibid.; Mathiesen 2012). Besides, although this broad definition encompasses the possibility of surveillance being used in a socially beneficial way, it also involves significant risks, such as intrusions on privacy and other civil rights as well as the potential to contribute to societal inequality, many of which are already considered a reality by current surveillance scholars (e.g. Lyon 2015; Fuchs 2008). Thus, in this article surveillance is seen as a serious social power warranting proper oversight and critical scrutiny.

Moreover, surveillance is a constantly changing phenomenon. It has been increasing exponentially in recent decades, and as digital technologies develop, new methods of surveillance continue to emerge (e.g. Lyon 2015). This development does not take place in a vacuum but is open to influence by citizens (see e.g. Lyon 2015: 138–140), politicians and, more broadly, nation states (e.g. Gorr and Schünemann 2013: 40). This highlights the importance and reformative potential of public discussions about the future of surveillance.

2.2 Discursive Struggles and the Media: A Critical Approach

To understand the discursive construction of meaning and its social implications, this article draws on a Foucauldian view of discourse (e.g. 1972; see below) and contemporary insights from the field of Critical Discourse Studies (CDS) (e.g. Wodak and Meyer 2016a; see, for instance, Hart and Cap 2014, van Dijk 2013 and Wodak and Meyer 2016b for the usefulness of this name for describing the field as opposed to the earlier Critical Discourse Analysis, *CDA*). Foucauldian discourse analysis and CDS provide a useful starting point, because they have a long tradition of examining the relations between language use, power and the structures that produce inequality (e.g. Wodak and Meyer 2016b; Blommaert 2005; cf. Foucault 1972), thus corresponding to the critical view of surveillance underlying the present study (see Simone 2009: 4 for the usefulness of CDA in analysing constructions of surveillance, cf. also Foucault 1977). CDS's contributions to the analysis of text and, particularly, media discourse also make it a fruitful theoretical and analytical framework for this article (e.g. Fairclough 1995; Richardson 2007).

Following Foucault (1972) and the core arguments of CDS, this article understands language use as a type of situated action that has social conditions and consequences (see e.g. Pietikäinen and Mäntynen 2009; Richardson 2007; Wodak and Meyer 2016b). In any given situation and society, language use can both help change and stabilize the social status quo (e.g. Wodak and Meyer 2016b: 7). Media discourse, as a prominent and powerful form of language use, is particularly important for constructing societal change (such as reforms relating to surveillance) as thinkable or unthinkable, possible or difficult (see below; cf. Fairclough 1995). The power that language use has on specific matters at a given moment can be understood through the concept of *discourses*, which are seen here as relatively stable ways of signifying and legitimizing topics and practices from specific points of view (Foucault 1972; also e.g. Pietikäinen and Mäntynen 2009), therefore "systematically form[ing] the objects of which they speak" (Foucault 1972: 49). Multiple discourses about a particular topic can be in circulation concurrently; some may dominate and some may be drowned out, but these hierarchies are continually contested (see Foucault 1972 for *order of discourse*, also e.g. Fairclough 1995). Consequently, media debates can and often do become sites of *discursive struggle* (cf. Wodak and Meyer ibid.: 12; Blommaert 2005: 4). This makes it possible for the media to both contribute to the stabilisation of prevailing social relations and to be transgressive and provide alternatives to them. Since the present article focuses on the highly controversial topic of surveillance and specifically on the media construction of possible solutions to the problems it poses, the socially constitutive and potentially transgressive characteristic of media debates is at the core of the article.

Although discursive struggles over surveillance can be found on various societal platforms, there is reason to claim that debates in traditional media platforms have special relevance for the present article. Firstly, even with the currently diminishing sales of newspapers worldwide, the media have retained a wide audience and can be considered a central institution exercising societal power (e.g. Burroughs 2015: 166; Richardson 2007). This means that Jäger's (2001: 49) contention that "the media regulate everyday thinking and exercise considerable influence on what is conductible and conducted politics" continues to be relevant. Secondly, although direct causal links between media coverage, institutions and society have been difficult to establish (McQuail 2007: 32; but see e.g. Resende 2013), there is plenty of research indicating that the media play an especially influential role in shaping public opinion and political decision making. For instance, research drawing on the agenda-setting theory has repeatedly shown how the media can focus public attention on specific issues and thus shape the political agenda (e.g. Graber 2007: 77). Thirdly, a connection between media coverage and policy has been established through interviews with policy makers (O'Heffernan 2007), and politicians' attempts to control the media also point to the political relevance of media discourse (e.g. Graber 2007). Fourthly, the media has also been acknowledged as an important societal actor specifically in relation to the future of surveillance, for instance by David Lyon (1994: 44, 177), who identifies journalism as a possible site of resistance to surveillance (see also Lischka 2015). As (some) traditional media platforms have been central actors in giving a voice to whistleblowers and making information in the Snowden documents available to the public, this contention seems to hold[1] (though see McGarrity 2011 for the limitations to the media's ability to perform its fourth estate role in the counter-terrorism context). Lastly and perhaps most importantly, previous research has highlighted the relevance of the media particularly for the types of questions explored by the present study: it has been concluded that among the most important ways the media can influence society are the media's abilities to direct attention to specific problems and solutions (McQuail 2007: 33), to function as a channel for persuasion and mobilisation (ibid.) and to narrow policy choices available to public officials (Graber 2007: 291). All of these insights, then, highlight the central role of media discussions for studying struggles over (and solutions to) surveillance.

Earlier research provides valuable insights into discursive struggles over surveillance and, therefore, into the premises on which criticism and possible solutions for surveillance may take place. Previous studies have found both the affirmation and contestation of surveillance in public discourse, and both standpoints are connected to recurring perspectives on surveillance and its effects. Pro-surveillance discourses tend to emphasise the importance of surveillance for national security (see e.g. Lischka 2015 and Barnard-Wills 2011 for British media surveillance discourse and Simone 2009 for US government discourse; cf. Qin 2015 for media frames of Edward Snowden and Salter 2015 for media frames of Glenn Greenwald), a standpoint which makes criticism difficult or redundant. The contestation of surveillance, on the other hand, has tended to rely on references to the loss of privacy and other civil rights (e.g. Barnard-Wills 2011; Lischka 2015). Much of the previous research has concentrated on Anglo-American public discourse, but there is reason to believe that the attitudes outlined above can also be found in cultures with a different relationship to surveillance (see above); in a previous paper examining discourses that (de)legitimise surveillance in the Finnish press, I found similar depictions of surveillance (Tiainen 2017). Critical voices do seem to be more dominant in the Finnish media than in the British media at least, but my article also had to conclude (paralleling Lischka's, ibid., insights on the British press) that overall the media criticism of surveillance has been constructed on a rather abstract and general level. The task of the present article, then, is to examine more closely those moments when surveillance is contested in order to gain a deeper understanding of the possibilities and limitations that media criticism poses for the future of surveillance.

---

[1]New media, of course, further enable dissenting voices to take part in public debates.

3   Data

The data consists of the first year of the Snowden coverage in *Helsingin Sanomat*, a
time frame which includes the most heatedly discussed revelations (at least in
Finland) and their aftermath. Since the newspaper puts its articles online, the data
was gathered from its digital archive with its own search engine, in two rounds:
first, using the queryterms *Edward Snowden, verkkovakoilu* (net espionage[2]) and
NSA, thus collecting all articles referencing the NSA scandal. Then, after a preliminary analysis which gave an initial impression of the relevant solutions, another
search was performed with additional terms to ensure that all articles clearly
continuing this discussion without reference to the Snowden case would be
included. The additional terms were *tietosuoja* (data protection), *tietoturva* (data
security) and *tiedustelu* (intelligence). Here, it became apparent that the Snowden
revelations were so topical that few articles omitted the connection, making the
demarcation of the data simple. The final data set consists of 619 articles and covers
a wide range of issues, from specific revelations (e.g. the Prism programme) to the
resulting political controversies and Snowden's asylum. Of course, many articles
concentrate on more tangentially related topics such as meetings between heads of
state and Nobel Prize nominees (Snowden was one in 2014). Most of the articles are
news articles, but opinion pieces (editorials, readers' letters and the like) also
appear. Online reader discussions, while clearly relevant to the public discourse
on surveillance, have been omitted from the analysis since they have a different
production process and different expectations for consumption (cf. e.g. Springer
et al. 2015); examining these is beyond the scope of this article.

Despite the overall ease of data demarcation, one notable exception must be
mentioned. The second search round brought out a scandal close to home—the
spying on the Finnish Ministry of Foreign Affairs, most intensely discussed in late
2013. This sparked demands to extend Finland's own surveillance capabilities
(which was already an ongoing process at that point), also at times constructed as
a solution to the problems discussed in the Snowden coverage. In a few articles, this
solution was discussed in a way that could be considered a response to both the
NSA and the Finnish scandals, and these were included in the data. However, I
decided to leave out articles where the topic was taken up only as a response to the
latter. This was based on the observation that the two scandals were discussed in
clearly different ways, with the NSA debate including lively contributions on the
legitimacy of global surveillance and considerations ranging from international
power relations to citizens' rights (which correspond to the concerns expressed
by surveillance scholars, see below), and the coverage of the Finnish espionage
affair typically displaying a much narrower perspective focused on preventing

---

[2]Helsingin Sanomat uses various key words as identifiers in categorizing articles in its digital
archive, and verkkovakoilu was a prominent one used in connection with articles referencing the
Snowden case.

future espionage on Finnish political bodies. Thus, solutions referring solely to this scandal would have addressed an altogether different problem.

4   Method

My analysis is an application of CDS, especially drawing on approaches concerned with the media and social actors (e.g. Fairclough 1995; van Leeuwen 2008). Starting with the (above described) understanding of the media discussion as a discursive struggle over surveillance, *solutions* relate to and rely on discourses that contest the justifications of surveillance (e.g. Tiainen 2017; Lischka 2015; Barnard-Wills 2011); they draw their relevance from the ways that surveillance is delegitimised but shift the focus from the level of criticising the present to outlining preferable futures and ways of moving forward. Thus, whereas strategies of *delegitimation* (cf. e.g. van Leeuwen 2008: 105–123) are essential in constructing surveillance as problematic, a *solution* is indispensable for constructing it as something that can be changed (see below). Therefore, solutions, which necessarily construct or imply an alternative to the present surveillance situation, can be powerful assets for delegitimizing discourses, and when it comes to speculating on the possible (political and other) consequences of the surveillance debate, they are significant. This conception of the way solutions contribute to discursive struggles guides my analysis and underlies the interpretation of the results.

For analytical purposes, I define a solution to be either a state or a situation that is constructed in the data as better than the current one or, alternatively, as an action that is depicted as a tool for reaching a better situation. This means that a solution may be both a means and an ends for solving the problem posed by surveillance. This is a choice I have made because differentiating between the two would often be extremely difficult, and they both meet the overall research interest in how a society might alter and improve the situation exposed by the revelations. Thus, solutions constitute a varied set of proposals and (represented) actions that are united by the function they serve in the discursive struggle. Consequently, they can at least potentially be constructed through a myriad of textual and other elements, the identification of which is an important part of the analytical process. Furthermore (and in accordance with the understanding described above of the connection between solutions and delegitimizing discourses), I will assume that an action or state of affairs can only be understood as a solution when the current situation is presented as problematic, meaning that the analysis focuses on articles where the surveillance revealed by Snowden is either implicitly or explicitly considered a problem by, at the very least, the actor responsible for evoking the solution (here, I will draw on previous studies concerned with delegitimation, e.g. Tiainen 2017; Lischka 2015). Lastly, although it would be tempting to include all kinds of (represented) critical reactions following the revelations as solutions—many of them can, after all, be expected to aim at some kind of change—I primarily understand a particular (re)action as a solution only when at least one actor in the article is depicted as considering it a way of improving the current situation. Without this delimitation, the analysis would unavoidably run into (for text analysis unanswerable) guesswork over the motives of the relevant actors.

Turning to the course of the analysis, I first mapped the data with the definition of 'solution' (described above) in mind and copied all occurrences, also noting how often they were presented as the main/starting theme of an article to get a sense of their overall prominence. It quickly became obvious that linguistic elements (as opposed to multimodal ones, e.g. pictures) were by far the most relevant for the analysis of solutions. The solutions were then categorised according to the type of change they proposed, and for an overview I also noted how often the solutions of each category appeared in the data and how they related to different types of actors (van Leeuwen's 2008: 23–25, sociologically oriented understanding of actors and agency was applied). This was followed by a close textual analysis of the relevant passages to investigate the ways solutions were discussed and how they related to the discursive struggle over surveillance. Finally, the possible societal implications of the results were explored (cf. e.g. Pietikäinen 2012: 420 for *zooming in* and *out*).

The next section is dedicated to the analysis. I will start with an overview of the way solutions generally appear and are constructed in the surveillance debate. After this, I will elaborate on the different types of solutions by dividing them into categories and subcategories. This is followed by an examination of the most relevant categories with examples,[3] with the emphasis on factors that regulate the power that solutions may have in the discursive struggle.

5   Overview of Solutions in the Surveillance Debate

As discussed above, for solutions to occur it is necessary for there to be something troubling about what Snowden revealed. The ensuing need for change gives the solutions their justification and relevance in the overall discursive struggle over surveillance, and it is therefore the backdrop against which the solutions must be understood and explored. In the current data, this (sense of) problem is linguistically articulated in many different ways (as will be shown in the example analyses below), but the underlying problem with surveillance remains the same across different types of solutions and throughout the news coverage. The solutions are related to an understanding of surveillance as a threat to citizens' privacy, to other civil rights and/or ultimately to democracy itself which, as earlier research has found (see below; e.g. Barnard-Wills 2011; Lischka 2015), is a common and powerful way of delegitimizing surveillance. In a previous analysis of *Helsingin Sanomat*, I called this logic *the discourse of threat* (Tiainen 2017). With such a

---

[3]The excerpts have been translated from Finnish into English by the author.

rationale behind them, the solutions in this data can typically be understood as more or less convincing proposals for bolstering democracy.

However, on the whole, solutions are not utilised in the data as a significant resource for challenging surveillance practices. This can already be seen in the position and space given to them in the newspaper articles: of the 619 articles that refer to the Snowden revelations, a solution constitutes the main/starting theme in only 39. The number is remarkably small compared to, for instance, the 130 articles that centre on Snowden's person and attempts to get asylum. When solutions are not a major theme in their respective articles, their content is frequently described in only a few sentences that appear in positions that are not very prominent (e.g. Fairclough 1995: 82). Further, they are often mentioned only vaguely and almost incidentally, not constructed as topics of ongoing societal or political debate in a way that would accumulatively deepen and specify the scope of the discussion (more below). Consequently, the way solutions are discussed often reduces their potential for providing credible alternatives to the present situation.

5.1   Solutions Categorised

The solutions discussed in the data can be divided into two categories, according to how directly they address surveillance practices. I will call the first category *next step* solutions. Such solutions are presented as preferred ways of moving forward from the current situation, without entailing any attempt to implement immediate change in practices directly related to surveillance. These include, for instance, expressing criticism of the USA or demanding clarification of Snowden's claims. The second category, which I will call *direct* solutions, covers solutions that do address practices relevant to the functioning of the surveillance process (e.g. legislation, using encryption), such as recommendations to create "Europe's own internet" or demands to stop espionage altogether.

To illustrate the range of solutions that appear within these two categories, I have further divided them into subcategories according to the type of action they discuss/ suggest. These are listed in Table 1, with simple and/or representative examples of each subcategory to give an indication of their realisations in the data.

Before moving on to detailed analyses, a brief overview is needed of the relative prominence of these categories and their connections to particular actor types in the data. Out of the two main categories, *direct* solutions is clearly the most prominent. Such solutions appear approximately three times as often as *next step* solutions, and they also occur more frequently in articles where a solution is the main theme. The subcategories overlap and converge to an extent that makes (quantitative) comparisons fruitless. Solutions overall are definitely brought up most often by journalists or other writers (e.g. in readers' letters), politicians, or interested parties (often experts; e.g. professors, civil servants). The global nature of the surveillance debate is strongly reflected in the assemblage of politicians and interested parties voicing solutions, with key actors such as Edward Snowden, Angela Merkel and Barack

Table 1 Solution categories

Solution category 1: Next step solutions	Solution category 2: Direct solutions
Action: Acquiring/demanding further information Example: "European institutions should immediately demand an explanation [on British surveillance practices]." (Statement attributed to German Minister of Justice Sabine Leutheusser-Schnarrenberger) (Pullinen 2013, June 24)	Action: Changing rules or regulations Example: "The [German] Chancellor suggested a joint European data protection law as a solution [to US espionage] (---)." (Kerola 2013, July 17)
Action: Having a societal/political discussion on surveillance Example: "Finland must actively participate in the international discussion on how to reconcile them [intelligence operations and the right to privacy]." (Limnéll 2013, June 13)	Action: (Working towards) Modifying or ending surveillance practices (no explicit references to legislative changes) Example: "It must be possible to control them [intelligence agencies] using parliamentary means, by the data protection authorities." (Statement attributed to Finnish Minister of the Environment Ville Niinistö) (Halminen 2013, June 16)
Action: Criticizing or reprimanding the surveillants Example: "Finland, the European Union and other countries should (---) tell the United States that we do not want them to be our big brother." (Viiri 2013, July 8)	Action: Using technical means of protection or otherwise improving security in technology use Example: "(---) [I]n the era of electronic surveillance, everyone should use encryption on the internet and in cell phones." (Statement attributed to Jacob Applebaum) (Sillanpää 2014, May 5)

Obama prominent among them. *Next step* solutions are proposed by all three actor types relatively evenly, whereas there is substantive variation in *direct* solutions according to subcategory. Interested parties, prominently technical experts, are behind many of the suggestions concerning *technical protection*, whereas *rules and regulations* as well as *modifying or ending surveillance practices* are dominated by politicians. The rare cases in which citizens appear in any capacity relating to solutions are concerned with *technical protection*. The relevance of these observations for the discursive struggle will be discussed below.

5.2   Solution Categories and the Discursive Struggle

The two main categories have different (potential) implications for the discursive struggle. *Next step* solutions give the actor suggesting them more leeway to leave the goal of the action/suggestion unspecified. Although these solutions can certainly constitute discursively powerful and practically useful tools for challenging surveillance (cf. e.g. Allmer 2012: 141; Lyon 2015: 138–140 for the importance of raising awareness and pressing for change), they also allow indefiniteness and finally evasion, which can reduce the transgressive potential of the delegitimizing discourse they relate to.

To exemplify how the indefiniteness of the *next step* solutions can function, I will briefly analyse an example from the subcategory of *public/political discussion* (see Excerpt 4 for an evasively used solution). It is also a good example to start with because, consisting only of one sentence, it illustrates the brevity and incidental nature of the solutions as I mentioned above (see Excerpt 3 for further discussion). This excerpt comes from an article that describes the British political debate after MI5 Director-General Andrew Parker criticised the Snowden revelations.

Excerpt 1

[Then Secretary of State for Business, Innovation and Skills Vince] Cable said in a BBC interview that political discussion is needed about the intelligence services' operations (Vasama 2013, November 10).

Here, the existence of a problem to be solved is implied with the verb *need*, and *political discussion* is identified as what is needed to improve the situation. The solution clearly belongs to the *next step* category since it would not necessarily have any impact on surveillance itself and the desired outcome is not defined (although a wish for change is implied). Typical of this subcategory, the passive verb, *is needed*, omits the actors responsible for making the change happen and thus "removes a sense of specificity from the clause" (Richardson 2007: 55), further highlighting the general and open-ended nature of the remark.

Since *direct* solutions necessarily involve some kind of change relating to surveillance itself, they require the purpose of the suggested line of action, or the nature of the desired situation, to be more clearly defined. In this sense, they have more potential for contributing to the struggle against surveillance, and their relative prominence in the data is an indication of the transgressive potential of the surveillance debate (there are limitations to this, though, as will be seen below). In fact, many of the solutions in this category are in line with suggestions that surveillance scholars have made to limit surveillance (cf. e.g. Lyon 2015: 140, 129). To introduce the category with an excerpt that exemplifies this transgressive potential, I will next present a solution that belongs to the subcategory of *technical protection* and is (unusually) specific about its motivations and preferred line of action. The excerpt comes from an article about Glenn Greenwald and his then newly published book about the Snowden leaks, *No Place to Hide*. It appears towards the end of the article and constitutes its only solution; therefore, although it clearly relates to the discursive struggle differently than the vague Excerpt 1, both exemplify the general tendency of solutions to be brief and rather inconspicuous.

Excerpt 2

Greenwald is confident that change will come through the internet companies and ordinary people taking precautions. He promises that when millions of people begin to use encrypted pgp emails, the NSA's resources will run out (Niskakangas 2014, May 28).

Here, the solution consists of both the means (people using encryption) and the desired end (NSA's resources running out). The existence of a problem is not stated explicitly in this excerpt, but the rest of the article (which is too long to include here) and Greenwald's widely broadcast criticism of the intrusions of surveillance on privacy and civil rights make it evident that surveillance is considered troublesome. This is also signalled here by the juxtaposition of positive words such as "confident" and "promise" with change and, concretely, encryption.

This example is typical of *technical solutions* in that it constructs a way for citizens to privately act against surveillance. Where it differs from most solutions in the data is in the element that gives it most strength in the face of a societal problem like surveillance: the suggestion that individual action can accumulate into collectively induced social change. In fact, in the subcategory of *technical protection*, meaningful private action and, therefore, solutions involving citizens as actors constitute about half of the data, although they rarely promise much more than protection for one individual's private email correspondence or something similar, along the lines shown in Excerpt 2. Thus, in characteristic occurrences in this subcategory, citizens are constructed as guardians of their own information but not as political actors (see example in Table 1), and so both action and goal tend to be limited to the private sphere. Consequently, the scope of the surveillance problem is also easily reduced to technical issues and attention is diverted from the social and political nature of the problem (cf. Lyon 2015: 134).

The tendency to exclude citizens as actors is even more pronounced in all the other subcategories, where citizens and normal net users are rarely mentioned at all. Citizens also seldom appear as actors making suggestions or demands in any category (cf. e.g. Fairclough 1995: 49 for the limited role of "ordinary people" as sources of information in the media generally). Since they nevertheless do appear in the data in other contexts, for instance as the unwilling targets of surveillance, this corresponds to what van Leeuwen (2008: 29) calls *backgrounding*, that is, the de-emphasising of specific actors in relation to a particular action. Altogether, this form of exclusion attributes a passive role to citizens and contributes to an understanding of the Snowden case as rather a spectacle for readers to follow than a societal issue to which they might contribute. Connected with the broader discursive struggle where precisely the societal importance of surveillance, such as its effects on civil rights, is emphasised, this role for citizens reduces the force of the transgressive discourse.

Solutions in the *direct* solutions category also lose power in other ways. Especially solutions from the often-overlapping subcategories of *rules and regulations* and *modifying or ending surveillance practices* tend to be discussed vaguely and sporadically, leading to their proposed plans of action often being little clearer than those in the *next step* category. This can be illustrated with the next example, representative of both subcategories and of their contribution to the discursive struggle in the data. The excerpt comes from an article discussing Finland's then foreign minister Erkki Tuomioja's speech at an annual gathering of Finnish ambassadors, where he defended Snowden and spoke against surveillance.

Excerpt 3

> 'The European Union, whose citizens and institutions have evidently also been the targets
> of illegal and inappropriate data collection, must act here clearly and openly in every
> direction to end and prevent the violations', Tuomioja said at the annual gathering of
> ambassadors. According to him, intervention in the violations of data security calls for strict
> international norms (Huhta and Raeste 2013, August 27).

Here, the existence of a problem needing a solution is clearly expressed by the
negative words referring to surveillance, such as "inappropriate" and "violation". It
would be possible to understand the recommendation to "act here clearly and
openly in every direction to end and prevent the violations" in the first paragraph
as a solution, indicated by the word "must" and belonging to the category of
modifying or ending surveillance practices (similar suggestions appear elsewhere
in the data and have been thus categorised). However, as this recommendation is
directly followed in the next paragraph by a reference to the more concrete need for
"international norms", I would rather interpret the latter as clarification for the
former, assigning the entire solution segment to the subcategory of *changing rules
or regulations*.

Although this solution includes both an ultimate goal (ending inappropriate
surveillance) and consideration of how to achieve this (international norms), its
formulation leaves the actual course of action open. The first paragraph only refers
to indeterminate (yet "open" and "clear") "action", while the second constructs the
"norms" as a type of mid-way goal that is "called for" in order for the aim to be
reached, thus omitting both the process by which the change should be achieved and
the actors responsible for making it happen. The vagueness about the necessary
course of action is a recurring characteristic of discussion relating to international
regulation, possibly a reflection of the difficulties involved in any such change,
which would require cooperation among a very broad range of perhaps unwilling
international actors. In any case, it makes alternative societal realities more difficult
to imagine.

Moreover, Tuomioja's statement is presented as isolated. Neither he himself
(as represented) nor the writer of the article embeds the comments into an ongoing
discussion about regulation, although similar suggestions have been made by
several prominent politicians (cf. Table 1 for an example), also covered in
Helsingin Sanomat. In this particular case, the isolation can partly be explained
by the article's focus on Tuomioja's speech at the ambassadors' meeting; however,
the isolated presentation of solutions runs throughout the data, particularly with
regard to politicians' suggestions (cf. Excerpt 1). Thus, the same suggestions keep
reappearing—international regulation is a good example—but the discussion rarely
proceeds from generalities to the actual steps that need to be taken. This keeps the
discussion on a superficial level and therefore reduces the suggestions' credibility.

I have now briefly discussed both the main solution categories and some
recurring characteristics that have consequences for their power to contribute to
the discursive struggle. This section will be concluded with one more example
which shows the interplay of various solutions and elaborates on an earlier (briefly)

mentioned characteristic of the *next step* category, that is, the potential to be strategically used for maintaining the impression of disapproval towards surveillance while actually discouraging action. The example comes from an article in which then Prime Minister Jyrki Katainen is interviewed about the revelation that the NSA has been tapping Angela Merkel's cell phone. I quote those paragraphs which are relevant for solutions, the first one coming from the beginning and the others forming the middle of the article.

Excerpt 4

1. None of us knows the truth about the matter. But of course every nation and also Europe as a whole considers this kind of news worrying, Katainen said to HS [*Helsingin Sanomat*] in Meise, outside Brussels, today, Thursday (Kähkönen 2013, October 24).
2. The free trade negotiations are terribly important for Europe, for our employment situation and economic development. I hope that (the suspicions) will not have (an impact), because Europe has an interest in getting the free trade agreement (Kähkönen 2013, October 24).
3. But of course we must get a full explanation of what has happened and we also need to be sure that this will not happen again, if it has happened (Kähkönen 2013, October 24).
4. According to Katainen, it is mainly up to Germany and the United States to sort this out (Kähkönen 2013, October 24).
5. The espionage scandal has also increased the EU's willingness to push forward new data protection legislation that is already being developed, which would improve the protection of personal data online (Kähkönen 2013, October 24).
6. A good question is how much it can affect espionage. Be that as it may, in all European countries people must [be able to] trust electronic services, electronic communication. These kinds of suspicions always shake this trust (Kähkönen 2013, October 24).

The clearest solution in this excerpt is getting "a full explanation" in paragraph 3, marked as an improvement by the expression "we must" and belonging to the main category of *next step solutions* and the subcategory of *acquiring further information*. This kind of demand is a recurring political reaction to the revelations in the data (cf. example in Table 1). Typically for its category, the solution does not involve a goal that would affect surveillance practices (also demonstrated in Excerpt 1), but one of sorts is given in the subsequent call for the "need to be sure that this will not happen again". However, the conditional "if it has happened" indicates that this is not relevant right now and highlights the need to wait, which is also prominently underlined both in the first sentence of paragraph 1 and by the repeated use of the hedging expression "suspicions" with reference to surveillance (paragraphs 2 and 6). This kind of caution can also be seen in the data in other politicians' statements; it could be interpreted as reflecting the difficult position countries face in confronting and attempting to solve a problem linked to a superpower like the USA.

Prime Minister Katainen's recurring emphasis on waiting not only justifies his call for more information but also implicitly deems any immediate action hasty, something that can also be seen in the way other possible (re)actions are discussed. In paragraph 5, "push[ing] forward Europe's data protection legislation" evokes what is a commonly appearing solution in the subcategory *rules and regulations* (cf. Merkel's suggestion in Table 1), although it is not clearly articulated as a solution here. In line with his reluctance for immediate action, Katainen questions the usefulness of the legislation (paragraph 6) and swiftly brings the discussion back to an abstract level with a generic remark about the importance of trust. Moreover, a far clearer rejection of any reaction (which is here not discussed as a solution, although elsewhere in the data it is) occurs in paragraph 2, where Katainen expresses a wish that the TTIP negotiations will not be disturbed by the revelations. The depiction of Katainen as prioritising the trade negotiations over acting on the surveillance scandal is particularly conspicuous because of the very specific account he gives of the importance of the TTIP agreement in stark contrast to the evasiveness with which problems related to surveillance are addressed. Further- more, his desire not to let the surveillance scandal jeopardise the TTIP negotiations is interesting because, at this point, there has been concern that the USA had used its intelligence to put the EU at a disadvantage in the negotiations. Katainen's com- ment disregards this possibility and therefore reduces the scope of the problem that might have to be solved (cf. Barnard-Wills 2009: 336–337 for the relevance of occluding linkages between surveillance practices).

The preference for refraining from action is also strengthened by the way Katainen is depicted as distancing himself (and thus, it could be argued, Finland as a nation) from the situation. While the international nature of the problem and, consequently, of probable solutions makes an emphasis on a joint answer from the European community understandable, the strategies that Katainen uses could be considered less a call for collective action than an attempt to shift responsibility. The distance is constructed in many ways: in paragraph 4, Katainen states explicitly that it is up to Germany and the USA to solve the problem. Paragraph 1 quotes Katainen saying "[n]one of us knows (---)", where the "us" establishes the problem as a general one, not something concerning Katainen as an individual (politician). In the following sentence, the expression "[b]ut of course every nation and also Europe as a whole…" further highlights the international scope of the problem. An additional level of distance is also constructed in the expres- sions "this kinds of news" (paragraph 1) and "these kinds of suspicions" (para- graph 6), which set the surveillance scandal in broader categories rather than constructing it as unique. Altogether, these portray Katainen as not responsible for suggesting or acting on solutions to surveillance. Similar if less conspicuous evasion can of course be interpreted in those demands for international action and regulation that fail to specify the actors and actual steps of proceeding (as in Excerpt 3).

Summing up, Excerpt 4 shows how a preference for the *next step* solution of *acquiring further information* is suggested, highlighted and complemented with a sense of distance in a way that makes concrete demands for action difficult and even unnecessary. This means that even a solution can function in ways that serve the status quo of surveillance instead of contributing to a discursive struggle to contest it.

6 Conclusion

Overall, the most conspicuous characteristic of the solutions appearing in the *Helsingin Sanomat* news coverage is that they tend to be brief and generic and are rarely the point of the article, therefore relatively seldom becoming subjects of constructive debate or critical evaluation. In other words, the dissenting voices in the surveillance debate focus more on criticizing the existing situation than finding alternatives to it. It can thus be said that the solutions, as voiced in the media, do not make a substantial contribution to the discursive struggle over surveillance.

The way different actors relate to the discussion of solutions may also restrict the potential of the criticism of surveillance. Citizens, and thus the expected readers of the newspaper, are rarely attributed an active role in finding a solution. This contributes to an understanding of surveillance as out of reach, as difficult to change. This is reinforced by the relative passivity of the Finnish political elite (at a level of societal decision-making the typical *Helsingin Sanomat* reader can influence by normal political participation). Politicians' suggestions for solving the situation tend to be (presented as) isolated comments rather than as parts of a political discussion aiming at change, and repeatedly these solutions are expressed with a lot of caution and hedging. The potential of political influence for setting limits to surveillance (cf. Gorr and Schünemann 2013: 40) therefore comes across in the data as restricted or remote. All of this further contributes to an understanding of surveillance as perhaps a negative societal power but a phenomenon that is beyond the normal sphere of societal and political decision-making, especially in the Finnish context.

The relatively superficial discussion on solutions in this data can perhaps be explained by *Helsingin Sanomat* being a general newspaper in which readers would not expect to find, for instance, detailed technical information. Besides, there are surely good reasons for the sense of distance and difficulty that characterise the potential attributed to Finnish citizens and even politicians to influence NSA surveillance. Nevertheless, these characteristics of the discussion consolidate the view of surveillance as distant and difficult to change and, especially due to the superficial level of discussion, restrict the extent to which readers can evaluate solutions and use the media discussion to make informed decisions, something which could be considered a central function of the media (e.g. Richardson 2007). This correlates with the conclusion of earlier studies that media discussions on surveillance often fail to go into the fundamentals of the problem, and tend to keep the discussion on a general level (Lischka 2015; Greenberg and Hier 2009; cf. Tiainen 2017).

References

Allmer, T. (2012). Critical internet surveillance studies and economic surveillance. In K. Fuchs Boersma, A. Albrechtslund, & M. Sandoval (Eds.), *Internet and surveillance. The challenges of web 2.0 and social media* (pp. 124–146). New York: Routledge.

Barnard-Wills, D. (2009). *The articulation of identity in discourses of surveillance in the United Kingdom*. University of Nottingham.

Barnard-Wills, D. (2011). UK news media discourses of surveillance. *The Sociological Quarterly, 52*, 548–567. doi:10.1111/j.1533-8525.2011.01219.x.

Blommaert, J. (2005). *Discourse: A critical introduction*. New York: Cambridge University Press.

Burroughs, E. (2015). Discursive representations of 'illegal immigration' in the Irish newsprint media: The domination and multiple facets of the 'control' argumentation. *Discourse & Society, 26*(2), 165–183. doi:10.1177/0957926514556029.

Fairclough, N. (1995). *Media discourse*. London: Edward Arnold.

Foucault, M. (1972). *The archaeology of knowledge*. London: Routledge.

Foucault, M. (1977). *Discipline and punish: The birth of the prison*. London: Penguin Books.

Fuchs, C. (2008). *Internet and society: Social theory in the information age*. New York: Routledge.

Gorr, D., & Schünemann, W. J. (2013). Creating a secure cyberspace–Securitization in Internet governance discourses and dispositives in Germany and Russia. *International Review of Information Ethics, 20*(12), 37–51.

Graber, D. A. (2007). *Media power in politics*. Washington, DC: CQ Press.

Greenberg, J., & Hier, S. (2009). CCTV surveillance and the poverty of media discourse: A content analysis of Canadian newspaper coverage. *Canadian Journal of Communication, 34*(3), 461.

Halminen, L. (2013, June 16). Ville Niinistö: The NSA whistleblower could get asylum in Finland. *Helsingin Sanomat*.

Hart, C., & Cap, P. (2014). *Contemporary critical discourse studies*. London: Bloomsbury.

Huhta, K., & Raeste, J. P. (2013, August 27). Tuomioja on whistleblowers: Manhunt incompatible with the principles of a constitutional state. *Helsingin Sanomat*.

Jäger, S. (2001). Discourse and knowledge: Theoretical and methodological aspects of critical discourse and dispositive analysis. In R. Wodak & M. Meyer (Eds.), *Methods of critical discourse analysis* (pp. 32–63). London: Sage.

Kähkönen, V. (2013, October 24). Katainen: Suspicions about the USA's cell phone spying are worrying. *Helsingin Sanomat*.

Kerola, P. (2013, July 17). Snooping scandal damages Merkel's reputation. *Helsingin Sanomat*.

Kumpu, V. (2016). On making a big deal. Consensus and disagreement in the newspaper coverage of UN climate summits. *Critical Discourse Studies, 13*(2), 1–15. doi:10.1080/17405904.2015.1042392.

Limnéll, J. (2013, June 13). Intelligence operations should not violate individual rights. *Helsingin Sanomat*.

Lischka, J. A. (2015). *Surveillance discourse in UK broadcasting since the Snowden revelations.* (Discussion Paper 12/2015). URL: http://www.zora.uzh.ch/116575/1/DCSS_Broadcasting-report%281%29.pdf

Lyon, D. (1994). *Electronic eye: The rise of surveillance society*. Minneapolis: University of Minneapolis Press.

Lyon, D. (2015). *Surveillance after Snowden*. Cambridge: Polity Press.

Mathiesen, T. (2012). Preface. In C. Fuchs, K. Boersma, A. Albrechtslund, & M. Sandoval (Eds.), *Internet and surveillance. The challenges of web 2.0 and social media* (pp. 15–20). New York: Routledge.

McGarrity, N. (2011). Fourth estate or government lapdog? The role of the Australian media in the counter-terrorism context. *Continuum: Journal of Media and Cultural Studies, 25*(02), 273–283.

McQuail, D. (2007). The influence and effects of mass media. In D. A. Graber (Ed.), *Media power in politics* (pp. 19–35). Washington, DC: CQ Press.

Niskakangas, T. (2014, May 28). The NSA battle is just beginning. *Helsingin Sanomat.*

O'Heffernan, P. (2007). Mass media roles in foreign policy. In D. A. Graber (Ed.), *Media power in politics* (pp. 294–305). Washington, DC: CQ Press.

Pietikäinen, S. (2012). Kieli-ideologiat arjessa. Neksusanalyysi monikielisen inarinsaamenpuhujan kielielämäkerrasta [Language ideologies in practice. A nexus analysis of multilingual Inari Sámi speaker's language biography]. *Virittäjä, 116*(3), 410–440.

Pietikäinen, S., & Mäntynen, A. (2009). *Kurssi kohti diskurssia* [Course towards discourse]. Tampere: Vastapaino.

Pullinen, J. (2013, June 24). Also British Intelligence reads messages from the net. *Helsingin Sanomat.*

Qin, J. (2015). Hero on twitter, traitor on news: How social media and legacy news frame Snowden. *International Journal of Press/Politics, 20,* 166–184. doi:10.1177/1940161214566709.

Resende, V. D. M. (2013). Media, sexual exploitation of children and the National Street Children's Movement in Brasília: An analysis of texts' social effects. *Critical Discourse Studies, 10*(3), 263–274. doi:10.1080/17405904.2013.791234.

Richardson, J. E. (2007). *Analysing newspapers: An approach from critical discourse analysis.* Basingstoke: Palgrave MacMillan.

Salter, L. (2015). Framing Glenn Greenwald: Hegemony and the NSA/GCHQ surveillance scandal in a news interview. *International Journal of Media & Cultural Politics, 11*(2), 183–201. doi:10.1386/macp.11.2.183_1.

Schulze, M. (2015). Patterns of surveillance legitimization: The German discourse on the NSA scandal. *Surveillance and Society, 13,* 197–217. URL http://library.queensu.ca/ojs/index.php/surveillance-and-society/index

Sillanpää, S. (2014, May 5). Expert: "Mobile phones are tracking devices that just happen to make phone calls". *Helsingin Sanomat.*

Simone, M. (2009). Give me liberty and give me surveillance: A case study of the US government's discourse of surveillance. *Critical Discourse Studies, 6,* 1–14. doi:10.1080/17405900802559977.

Springer, N., Engelmann, I., & Pfaffinger, C. (2015). User comments: Motives and inhibitors to write and read. *Information, Communication and Society, 18*(7), 798–815.

Tiainen, M. (2017). (De)legitimating electronic surveillance: A critical discourse analysis of the Finnish news coverage of the Edward Snowden revelations. *Critical Discourse Studies.*

Van Dijk, T. A. (2013). *CDA is NOT a method of critical discourse analysis.* Associacion de Estudios sobre Discurso y Sociedad. Accessed May 7, 2016, from http://www.edisoportal.org/debate/115-cda-not-method-critical-discourse-analysis

Van Leeuwen, T. (2008). *Discourse and practice: New tools for critical discourse analysis.* Oxford: Oxford University Press.

Vasama, T. (2013, November 10). Espionage discussion heats up late in Britain. *Helsingin Sanomat.*

Viiri, K. (2013, July 8). Finland must oppose snooping. *Helsingin Sanomat.*

Wodak, R., & Meyer, M. (2016a). *Methods of critical discourse studies.* Los Angeles: Sage.

Wodak, R., & Meyer, M. (2016b). Critical discourse studies: History, agenda, theory and methodology. In R. Wodak & M. Meyer (Eds.), *Method of critical discourse studies* (pp. 1–22). Los Angeles: Sage.

The Unshaken Role of GCHQ

The British Cybersecurity Discourse After the Snowden Revelations

Stefan Steiger

1 Introduction

When Edward Snowden revealed the extensive internet surveillance carried out by both the National Security Agency (NSA) and the British Government Communications Headquarter (GCHQ), he sparked far-reaching debates about appropriate state behaviour in cyberspace. The governments of the US and UK faced harsh criticism following the first revelations in June 2013. Although both states were accused of extensive surveillance activities, reactions after the revelations differed considerably in both countries. While the Obama administration enacted some legal measures to limit the NSA's spying on US citizens (i.e. USA Freedom Act) after facing not only external but also domestic criticism, in the UK there has been no such legislation and much less domestic debate about state surveillance.

Even among the British public, trust in intelligence agencies remained relatively high following the revelations. In a public opinion poll, conducted in January 2015, more than 60% of respondents expressed their trust in intelligence agencies (Fig. 1). Not only have there been hardly any changes in GCHQ's surveillance practices, the Investigatory Powers Act, that came into force in November 2016, even legalised some of the practices revealed by Edward Snowden and increased surveillance capabilities (Schafer 2016). The Act faced substantial opposition from NGOs during its drafting phase; critics argued that "the Bill will give the UK one of the most extreme surveillance laws in the world" (EDRi 2016). Concerns have also been raised by the UN's special rapporteur on the right to privacy, Joseph Cannataci, who emphasised the fact that the UK may set a bad example. He encouraged

S. Steiger (✉)
Heidelberg University, Bergheimer Str. 58, 69115 Heidelberg, Germany
e-mail: stefan.steiger@ipw.uni-heidelberg.de

© Springer International Publishing AG 2017
W.J. Schünemann, M.-O. Baumann (eds.), *Privacy, Data Protection and Cybersecurity in Europe*, DOI 10.1007/978-3-319-53634-7_6

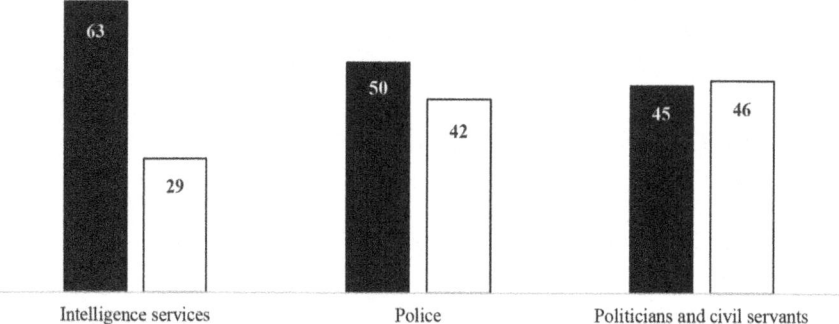

To what extent, if at all, would you trust the following to behave responsibly with information obtained using new surveillance powers? %

■ Trust □ Do not trust

Intelligence services   Police   Politicians and civil servants

Fig. 1 Limited trust in surveillance institutions' behaviour. Source: https://yougov.co.uk/news/2015/01/18/more-surveillance-please-were-british/ [14.11.2016]

> [...] the UK Government to take this golden opportunity to set a good example and step back from taking disproportionate measures which may have negative ramifications far beyond the shores of the United Kingdom (UN 2016: 14).

The Snowden revelations also sparked opposition from the European Parliament (EP 2014, 2015). The move towards a more extensive surveillance regime is even more surprising considering the fact that GCHQ's surveillance activities, like the now infamous Tempora program (Corera 2015: 337), were more invasive and less controlled than the NSA's. Thus, Edward Snowden called GCHQ's spying even worse than that of its American counterpart.

> GCHQ has much less strict legal restrictions than other western government intelligence. [...] They enjoy authorities that they really shouldn't be entitled to. And the problem with that is, when you have an unrestrained intelligence agency that's not being well overseen, that's not accountable to the public, they're going to go further than they need to. They're going to overreach (Snowden 2014).

This chapter therefore addresses the following question: how was it possible for GCHQ's surveillance practices to remain stable after the Snowden revelations? It seems that fears of an overreaching or so-called 'deep state' have not been shared by British policymakers, and this did not change after the Snowden revelations.

Following the disclosures, scholars focused on, inter alia, their potential impact (Penney 2016; Stahl 2016; Bauman et al. 2014), the legal dimension of internet surveillance (Ni Loideain 2015; Joergensen 2014), questions of accountability (Bakir 2015), the particular importance of internet companies (Moran 2016) or on the enabling technical infrastructure (DeNardis 2015). Only few studies touched upon the politics facilitating the surveillance practices (see Dimmroth and Schünemann 2017; Schulze 2015). This chapter examines why the UK reacted so affirmatively towards disclosed surveillance measures and GCHQ following the Snowden revelations.

Some scholars might answer this with reference to the terrorist threat. However, while this is crucial to understanding the installation of the extensive surveillance programmes, it does not fully explain the different policy choices, since there seems to be a more or less similar threat perception in the US and the UK (OSCE Network 2014; Kirchner and Sperling 2007). Another argument might point towards the great dependence on the internet economy in the US, but given the fact that the UK maintains the biggest digital economy in relation to GDP in the G20 (Boston Consulting Group 2015), and considering that some of those companies also sued the UK Government over revealed surveillance practices (*The Guardian* 2014), this explanation isn't convincing either. The limited influence of US-based internet companies is further reflected in the fact that they criticised surveillance in its entirety, but the government enacted restrictions only for surveillance of US citizens.

This article argues that this policy is best understood by looking at the historical experiences the Britons have made with their intelligence agencies. This study conducts a role theoretical analysis of the domestic processes of role contestation or role stabilisation in the light of revealed surveillance practices. The most important interactions in this regard took place between GCHQ itself, the UK Government and Parliament. Although the harshest criticism was expressed by the media outlets involved in the revelations (e.g. *The Guardian*), some critical voices calling for a re-evaluation of the established system could also be heard from members of the Government (Clegg 2014). Since government and parliament hold the legal power to control and change GCHQ's role, their support was crucial to maintaining established intelligence policies.[1] Therefore, this study will analyse the reactions of GCHQ, government and parliament following the Snowden revelations.

To answer the research question, the article will proceed in four steps. First, the role theoretical framework will be developed; a particular focus will thereby lie on the importance of the historical self. In order to identify GCHQ's historical role, the following section will shed light on the British experiences with intelligence agencies and the history of GCHQ in particular. This part will also provide a short insight into the British culture of secrecy. In the fourth section, the interpretative analysis takes place. A final conclusion sums up the findings.

2 Role Theory, Domestic Politics and the Historical Self

Originating in social psychology and symbolic interactionism (Mead 1962; Blumer 1969), the analytical concept of social roles also gained influence in the study of International Relations. Starting with Kalevi Holsti's seminal work on "National

---

[1]Regarding the judiciary, relevant judgments will be addressed briefly where necessary.

Role Conceptions in the Study of Foreign Policy" (1970), more and more research made use of roles as analytical tools to analyse foreign policies.

Following a symbolic interactionist reading of role theory, roles are considered to be "social positions [...] that are constituted by ego and alter expectations regarding the purpose of an actor in an organized group" (Harnisch 2011: 8). Roles are conceptualised as relational social constructs. As such, they are always related to so called counter-roles (protector—protectee; McCourt 2012). Stable social relations emanate only when roles and counter-roles 'match'—i.e. when they are commensurable. If one actor doesn't accept the social setting, he may contest the role(s) of other actors in order to change the social structure. Applied to the situation following the Snowden revelations, this means that actors could (and especially NGOs actually did) contest the disclosed practices in order to change the social role relationship between governments and citizens. This process of role contestation may be initiated by foreign or domestic actors.

Role theory in International Relations long acted on the assumption of stable and (domestically) uncontested roles. The process of role formation and possible conflicts surrounding this process were of no concern. This changed in recent years. Since then, role theoreticians have focused increasingly on the process of domestic role contestation and have thereby begun to analyse the sphere of domestic politics more thoroughly (Cantir and Kaarbo 2012; Wehner and Thies 2014; Brummer and Thies 2015; Harnisch 2015; Kaarbo 2015).

Since both the US and the UK faced significant criticism from foreign actors (arguably the UK faced even more external opposition, i.e. from the EU) but only the US enacted restraints on internet surveillance, it is reasonable to focus on the domestic process of role contestation/stabilisation in the UK. This article analyses the discourse of GCHQ, government and parliament in order to understand what enabled such an extensive surveillance regime and its resilience.

To analyse the domestic interactions this study suggests that a role play is not taking place exclusively in relationships between states on the international level (for example Thies 2013). Instead, the international role play is analytically supplemented by a domestic role play between GCHQ, government and parliament. This study analyses the process that enabled GCHQ to maintain its role as 'informant' protecting the UK, equipped with far-reaching surveillance capabilities.

This article argues that the reconfirmation of GCHQ's role through commensurable counter-role-taking from government and parliament was made possible by a particularly positive historical conception of GCHQ. From this perspective, the stability of GCHQ's far-reaching spy practices is best understood by looking at the UK's historical experiences with its intelligence agencies. In this regard, this article draws on studies emphasising the importance of historical experiences for the process of self-identification and, therefore, role-taking (Harnisch 2016a, b). The so-called historical self is considered to be crucial for the handling of foreign policy and may serve as a positive or negative reference point (Harnisch 2016a: 11–13). In the case of the UK, it is argued that the stable role of GCHQ is enabled by a mostly positive perception of the agency, especially with reference to its predecessor, the Government Code & Cipher School (GC&CS). The importance of the historical self in the process of self-identification is emphasised by some role theoreticians. For China, it is argued that the role performed by the PRC is dependent on the historical self that is invoked (i.e. victim; Harnisch 2016b). Historical selves therefore serve as reference points and guide the process of role-taking.

In line with this, it is argued that the historical self is also at play at the domestic level of role contestation or stabilisation. Leading representatives of GCHQ invoked its (positive) historical experiences in most public statements. They especially made reference to GCHQ's predecessor. This portrayed image was shared by the government and most parts of parliament. It is this relation that helps best to understand the far-reaching spy activities and their stability. The study thereby also contributes to the "few studies [that; *author's note*] have examined the effects of historical self-identification on current role taking or role making behavior" (Harnisch 2016a: 6).

In order to assess the different role conceptions and a potential role contestation, a discourse analysis of debates about the Snowden revelations was conducted, focussing on the period from June 2013 (first revelations) to March 2016. The corpus encompasses documents from GCHQ, government and parliament.

3 British Intelligence Agencies as '(Faithful) Informants': A Brief Historical Overview

In 1919, the Government Code and Cypher School (GC&CS), located at Bletchley Park, was founded as Britain's signal intelligence agency. In 1946, it was renamed to its present name, the Government Communications Headquarter. The existence of GCHQ was officially disclosed to the public in 1994, when the Intelligence Services Act established the legal framework for the work of GCHQ and the Secret Intelligence Service (SIS/MI6). The work of the Security Service (MI5) had been put on a legal basis only five years before that in 1989 (Bochel et al. 2015). Compared to other Western democracies, the existence of intelligence agencies was officially admitted rather late in the UK. That doesn't mean that there had been no disclosures about intelligence practices before that time, but in contrast to other states (e.g. the US), far-reaching revelations were scarce. Scholars have argued that investigative journalism in the UK was hampered by legal restrictions such as the Official Secrets Act (OSA, first passed in 1889 and amended in 1911) and the system of D-Notices (introduced in 1912) (Thomas 1991; Sadler 2001). Both are designed to prevent the disclosure of secret information, making the work of journalists especially difficult. Although there have been some disclosures about intelligence failures and times when the system of secrecy was contested by journalists, for example during the D-Notice affair in 1967 or during the ABC affair in 1977/1978, none of those led to far-reaching critiques of the intelligence agencies. Criticism focused more on the extensive amount of secrecy surrounding the agencies than on the agencies themselves. In contrast, US intelligence agencies suffered from substantial critique during the 1960s and 1970s. Revelations about the Watergate scandal, the Bay of Pigs disaster and the plotted assassination of Fidel Castro led to discussions about the secret practices of intelligence services (Halperin et al. 1976). As a result, the US Government reformed parts of the intelligence legislation. While the US reduced political influence on the agencies, which was seen as a major source of failure, the British Wilson administration took another path and maintained political influence, especially through the Joint Intelligence Committee (JIC) (Jeffreys-Jones 2013: 143).

Despite not doing any 'better' than their American counterparts, British agencies were able to maintain a positive reputation throughout the twentieth century. This positive perception was enabled by legislation such as the OSA, but it was also based on narratives describing British intelligence agencies as 'faithful informants' protecting the empire; those arguments were most frequent between 1910 and 1930 (Jeffreys-Jones 2013: 52). This view was further facilitated by the disclosure of the so-called 'Ultra Secret'. These factors laid the foundation for a powerful conception that is still resonating in political discourse today. Activities of the GC&CS during World War II remained secret until 1974, when Frederick Winterbotham, a former Group Captain of the Royal Air Force, published 'The Ultra Secret', revealing that GC&CS was able to break German encryption in January 1940. The book was met with significant public interest. For the first time, light was shed on the work of the codebreakers located at Bletchley Park. Furthermore, it showed the public the enormous importance of the resulting information advantage and the influence this had in ending the war (Jeffreys-Jones 2013). This revelation had substantial impact on the agency's reputation. GC&CS's success during the Second World War

> [. . .] has become a common touchstone for popular culture—celebrated both on the printed page and on the silver screen. Its gifted practitioners became a shorthand term for community, triumph over adversity, even the idea of Britishness itself (Moran 2013: 256).

It is this historical experience that is frequently invoked by representatives of GCHQ and that is shared and accepted by large parts of government and parliament when discussing the Snowden revelations.

Apart from historical experience, there is another feature of the British intelligence agencies that sustained their good reputation. Scholars from Intelligence Studies sometimes highlight a difference between the American and British ways of approaching intelligence (Davies 2002).

> [. . .] in the United States 'information' is a component of 'intelligence' while in the UK, 'intelligence' is a particular type of information. This is not merely a semantic difference: it has profound and pervasive institutional implications (Davies 2004: 500).

In role theoretical terms, this emphasises a difference in the functional scope of the spy agencies' roles. This distinction is also important to understanding the reputation of GCHQ. GCHQ's function for the group (the state) is more narrowly defined than that of other intelligence services, e.g. the NSA. GCHQ's task is more or less limited to information gathering. The analysis and assessment of this information takes place in other, more politically involved institutions such as JIC, which is part of the Cabinet Office (Gibson 2009). The narrow functional scope of the role is also expressed by members of the Government:

> The purpose of secret intelligence is to fill in the blanks where the picture created by more conventional means remains incomplete; and to provide illumination to spaces that are otherwise completely dark to us—allowing us to get an appreciation of what is at the other side of the hill (Philip Hammond 2015).

GCHQ's own role conception also reflects this functional limitation and explicitly emphasises the focus on information gathering (Lobban 2013).

The difference in functional scope might have been crucial for the agency to maintain its reputation, since intelligence failures were therefore often not attributed to the agency alone, but split between involved institutions. The Butler Report, which investigated the 'intelligence failure' that led to the military intervention in Iraq in 2003, may serve as an example for this. In the Report, the chairman of the JIC took a substantial portion of the criticism (Phythian 2009: 17). The historical experience as well as the functional scope of GCHQ's role have facilitated a particularly positive conception of the agency. This perception strongly resonated in the discourse following the Snowden revelations.

4 Interpretive Analysis

4.1 We Are the Good Guys: GCHQ's Reactions to the Revelations

Immediately after the disclosures, representatives of GCHQ made more public statements than usual in order to reassure the public and policymakers of their vital work. Furthermore, the agency significantly increased its public relations activities and granted unprecedented access to journalists (*The Guardian* 2015).

In most public statements, two main points of reference can be found. The first is the reference to the historical self of the agency, namely the GC&CS (often referred to as Bletchley Park) and the historical achievements attained. Secondly, this is often combined with an analogy of the threats the UK faced in the past and emerging new threats in the digital age. These arguments were regularly proposed to maintain the policies surrounding the agency; furthermore, they are an expression of the role conception held by GCHQ.

Sir Iain Lobban, then director of GCHQ, directly addressed the historical dimension of the agency's task in a speech given at the Annual Defence and Security Dinner in November 2013.

> I've already spoken about the rich legacy of Bletchley Park for GCHQ: just as the work at Bletchley involved exploiting the adversary's information risk whilst minimising our own, today's internet provides a virtual battlespace for a similar struggle (Lobban 2013).

By invoking the historical achievements of GCHQ's predecessor and comparing the challenges the UK faced back in the 1930s and 1940s to the ones faced in the digital age, Lobban emphasised the importance of the intelligence community. He further stretched this point by mentioning the meaning of the gathered information for the British military (Lobban 2013).

The pattern of invoking the historical legacy and highlighting historical analogies can be found in most statements given by GCHQ representatives. Another example directly links the GC&CS's success during the Second World War to the current work of its successor.

> I am proud to say that our security mission now stands alongside the intelligence mission, once again on equal terms as it was during World War Two. It is these extraordinary people who were out there, banging the information assurance drum, before cyber security became rather fashionable (Lobban 2014a).

Lobban emphasized the fact that the UK still needs GCHQ as an 'informant' to ensure national security. The role didn't lose any of its relevance over time.

> In another dark time, a sparkling generation radiated their genius from dingy huts at Bletchley to defend a beleaguered nation against the Nazi onslaught: They sent the intelligence to leaders right here in these War Rooms. Just as today, GCHQ continues to supply our National Security Council with the intelligence necessary to make the right strategic decisions (Lobban 2014b).

These arguments and analogies were also referred to by Lobban's successor, Robert Hannigan (2015), and colleagues such as Ciaran Martin, Director General Cyber Security of GCHQ (Martin 2015).

These statements exemplify a pattern that can be found in most documents published by GCHQ. They show that, in the time following the Snowden revelations, GCHQ tried to highlight its crucial task to ensure security in the UK in the digital age. Its representatives did so by frequently invoking its predecessor's historic achievements and by directly comparing the current challenges to those of the 1930s and 1940s. This shows not only a move to establish a legacy and to emphasise historic continuity, but also an attempt to convince others of the dangers stemming from cyberspace. The revelations did not spark a process of re-evaluation of established policies. Instead GCHQ tried to justify its own role and tried to portray the applied practices as necessary to combat threats emanating from cyberspace. GCHQ's representatives did so by heavily drawing on the positive historical self of the agency. The leaked information or the name Edward Snowden are hardly ever mentioned in any statement by GCHQ representatives.

4.2 Surveillance Is Necessary and Well Scrutinised: Government's Reactions to the Revelations

Government's first reaction to the revelations was to condemn the leaked information as a harm to the security of the UK. This is exemplified by a statement of then Foreign Secretary William Hague:

> The Government deplores the leaking of any classified information wherever it occurs. Such leaks can make the work of maintaining the security of our own country and that of our allies more difficult. And by providing a partial and potentially misleading picture they give rise to public concerns (William Hague 2013).

Following the first revelations, the government even tried to prevent further disclosures by forcing journalists to physically destroy hard disks containing leaked documents (*The Guardian*2013). Rejections of the Snowden revelations have been a common theme in governmental statements since then and were shared across departments.

> The people who work at GCHQ do fantastic work—it is a centre of brilliant expertise and knowledge; they do difficult work away from the public gaze, and any comments that seem to undermine what they do in the service of national security has to be strongly deprecated (Francis Maude, Con; HoC 2015a: 1319).

The government continued to justify the disclosed practices as proportionate and appropriately controlled. Members of the government mainly relied on three arguments to stabilise GCHQ's role as informant and retain the revealed practices. The first argument claims that established democratic control over the intelligence agencies is far reaching and thereby denies the "danger of a 'deep state'" (William Hague 2013). Secondly, the need for surveillance capabilities was justified by highlighting the current threats to the UK, especially the potential risks posed by terrorist attacks. Thirdly, these arguments were combined in reference to the positive image of GCHQ and its employees, thereby relating to the historical reputation of the agency.

Speaking to the House of Commons (HoC) directly following the first revelations in June 2013, then Foreign Secretary William Hague emphasised the strict control over GCHQ as well as the good reputation of the signal intelligence agency:

> It is vital that we have this framework of democratic accountability and scrutiny. But I also have nothing but praise for the professionalism, dedication and integrity of the men and women of GCHQ. I know from my work with them how seriously they take their obligations under UK and international law. [...] if they [the citizens; *author's note*] could witness the integrity and professionalism of the men and women of the intelligence agencies, who are among the very finest public servants our nation has, then I believe that they would be reassured by how we go about this essential work (William Hague 2013).

Additionally, then Prime Minister David Cameron highlighted the historic achievements as well as the crucial task of the intelligence agencies.

> We have every reason to be proud of our intelligences [*sic!*] services and the way in which they are properly constituted in this country. [...] We owe them—and every intelligence officer in our country—an enormous debt of gratitude. These silent heroes and heroines are keeping our country safe. They deserve our wholehearted support (David Cameron 2013).

The positive image of GCHQ was also stressed by other members of the government. The case for strong surveillance capabilities was mostly made with reference to the terrorist threat to the UK (Hammond 2015).

Most members of the government stressed the work of the agencies as being crucial and defended and stabilised the uncovered practices. Although there have been some critics, especially among Liberal Democrats (Clegg 2014), the government was quick in taking a commensurable counter-role in order to uphold the spy policies as they were revealed.

A major challenge to this policy came in a judgement from the Court of Justice of the European Union (CJEU) which declared the Data Retention Directive illegal in April 2014 (CJEU 2014). Since this decision also questioned data retention practices in the UK, the government felt the need to put data retention on new legal ground. Then Home Secretary Theresa May called for immediate action:

> If we delay, we face the appalling prospect that police operations will go dark, trails will go cold and terrorist plots will go undetected. If that happens, innocent lives may be lost (HoC 2014: 717).

Following a short debate, the Data Retention and Investigatory Powers Act was quickly run through parliament with little contestation (DRIPA 2014).[2] While members of the government argued that DRIPA's only purpose was to maintain existing capabilities (HoC 2014: 704–755), critics stressed the fact that DRIPA introduced new, extraterritorial powers (Open letter 2014). But this critique didn't gain enough power to actually change any of the proposed surveillance policies. Again, the government managed to counter criticism by highlighting GCHQ's positive historical role, which was hardly contested domestically (some exceptions can be found in the counter-role-taking of Parliament in the next section). The most influential contestation against DRIPA emanated from a judgement from the High Court of Justice, that considered parts of the legislation to be violating EU law (HCoJ 2015) and obligated the Government to enact a new legal framework.

Given the fact that GCHQ is a government agency, it comes as no surprise that the work of the agency was considered legitimate and necessary. By proposing and adopting DRIPA, the Government arguably did not only stabilise revealed intelligence practices but even extended some surveillance capabilities.[3]

4.3   Torn Between Praise and Criticism: Parliament's Reaction to the Revelations

The first debate concerning the revelations in the House of Commons took place on 10 June 2013. This debate mostly emphasised the important work of GCHQ, and praise for the agency was expressed by most parties. This view is exemplified by the following statements:

> All our constituents should be grateful for the work of the Security Services, and some will owe their lives to their professionalism (Henry Bellingham, Con) (HoC 2013: 42).

---

[2]To ensure support from opposition, DRIPA was enacted containing a sunset clause.

[3]Arguably surveillance capabilities were also extended by the Counter-Terrorism and Security Act 2015.

The positive perception was also shared by most Labour MPs.

> I begin my remarks by echoing the words of the Foreign Secretary and put on record the support and admiration of the whole House for the important—indeed, vital—work that is done by our country's intelligence and security services. Theirs is some of the most important but inevitably least recognised work undertaken to protect the security of our nation, and it is right that we take the opportunity to offer our thanks and praise for their efforts (Douglas Alexander, Lab) (HoC 2013: 34).

Furthermore, the historic importance of intelligence and the success of GC&CS was stressed by some MPs:

> Veterans of Bletchley Park, like my own parents, were and are widely described as heroes for the secret victories that we can now talk about, they having kept their secrets for many decades. Does the Foreign Secretary agree that GCHQ, as Bletchley's successor, does equally vital but equally secret work [...] (Martin Horwood, LD) (HoC 2013: 38).

Though historic references mostly focused on the time of the Second World War, some MPs invoked events even further back in time.

> Has not our national security relied for centuries on the effective intercept of communications? The Spanish armada was said to have been averted as much by the pen of Francis Walsingham as by the Royal Navy. Surely what has changed is the nature of those communications. The threat to the public comes not from the intelligence agencies, which have no interest at all in the communications of members of the public [...] (Nick Herbert, Con) (HoC 2013: 44).

But the positive historical perception did not remain uncontested during the debate. Some MPs made critical reference to negative historical events and questioned the often proposed benignity of GCHQ. This view was shared by parts of the Liberal Democrats, the Scottish National Party, the Greens and some Labour MPs.

> The Cathy Massiter[4] case proved that, 50 years after the last war, intensive surveillance of peace activists, trade unionists and left-wing parties had failed to turn up a single spy, but it was discovered that in that same period, more than 20 members of the Secret Intelligence Service were spying for the Soviet Union. Since then, we have had untruths on weapons of mass destruction and a Government cover-up to this House on the handing over of prisoners to oppressive regimes to be tortured. Is the Foreign Secretary telling us today that the only people now under surveillance are the guilty? (Paul Flynn, Lab) (HoC 2013: 46).

This example shows that there are also negative historical reference points with regard to British intelligence agencies, but this perception was not shared widely and didn't gain enough traction to actually change established policies.

Following this debate, there have been several inquiries concerning the revealed practices of GCHQ. Two of them were conducted by parliamentary committees, namely the Intelligence and Security Committee (ISC) and the Home Affairs Committee (HAC). The ISC was established under the Intelligence Service Act 1994 and became a statutory committee of parliament in 2013; its task is to scrutinise the work of the intelligence agencies (Bochel et al. 2015). In a first

---

[4]Cathy Massiter was a member of MI5 and disclosed surveillance activities of the agency in the 1980s.

statement immediately following the disclosures, the ISC assured that GCHQ was not breaking any laws (ISC 2013) but also announced a comprehensive review of the legal framework. In the aftermath of the revelations and during the subsequent inquiry, the ISC held public hearings for the first time in its history. The resulting report was published in March 2015 and provided a more nuanced and partly critical view on surveillance provisions. The ISC still built on and defended the good reputation of GCHQ; the report did not address possible misconduct by the agency. It also stressed the importance of maintaining bulk internet surveillance capabilities. The report concluded:

> We are satisfied that the UK's intelligence and security Agencies do not seek to circumvent the law [. . .] However, that legal framework has developed piecemeal, and is unnecessarily complicated. We have serious concerns about the resulting lack of transparency, which is not in the public interest (ISC 2015: 2).

The ISC thereby switched reference points from the agency itself to the legal framework governing surveillance activities. It tasked the government with a complete revision of the legal regime that regulates surveillance practices. The report from the HAC was even more critical concerning the legal provisions surrounding the established surveillance practices, but remained positive on GCHQ (HAC 2014). The call for a new legal framework was also shared by the Independent Reviewer of Terrorism Legislation, David Anderson (IRoTL 2015). Subsequently, the government began to work on a new legal basis to replace old provisions established by the Regulation of Investigatory Powers Act (RIPA).

Debate about this new legal framework ended with the passing of the Investigatory Powers Act in November 2016. A first reading of the Draft Investigatory Powers Bill took place in November 2015. The new legal framework extends surveillance capabilities even further. Although those plans were first met with considerable scepticism, the positive image of GCHQ also resonated in this debate. However, this time it was advised by some MPs to put the obligation on the government to establish a legal framework that is suitable for the work of GCHQ.

> Constituents of mine who work at GCHQ are some of the most talented and dedicated public servants anywhere in our country, but they are also conscientious and scrupulous about acting within the law. Does the Secretary of State agree that these measures contain a clear authorisation and oversight framework, including a welcome judicial element, which can command public confidence and, crucially, allow GCHQ employees to do their vital work with professionalism and pride? (Alex Chalk, Con) (HoC 2015b: 982).

Following this debate, the draft was scrutinised by three parliamentary committees: the Science and Technology Committee (STC 2016), the Joint Committee (JC 2016) and the ISC (2016), all of which advised major revisions to the draft. The government claimed to have addressed all those issues in a new draft, which was discussed in the House of Commons in March 2016, but the legislation still faced opposition from Liberal Democrats, SNP and the Greens, while Labour MPs abstained from voting and even among Conservatives it was not unanimously applauded:

[...] The fact that a particular power might never, to our knowledge, have been misused does not mean that we should disregard the possibility of creating transparent safeguards for its use, if this can be done without interfering with operational capability. We also have to accept the possibility that times might change and standards slip (Dominic Grieve, Con) (HoC 2016: 837).

To sum up, debates in the House of Commons immediately following the revelations mostly reflected a positive perception of GCHQ. This enabled the uncovered practices to be maintained, and GCHQ's capabilities remained untouched. Parliament was also quick in accepting DRIPA, in debates surrounding the Draft Investigatory Powers Bill there was more resistance to proposed plans. But in the end the Bill was passed by the House of Commons and the Investigatory Powers Act came into force in November 2016.

5   Conclusion

This chapter shed light on the surprising stability of extensive British surveillance policies after the Snowden revelations. It argued that this stability was enabled by the positive perception of the British signal intelligence agency which was shared among most decision makers. The analysed documents showed that GCHQ itself tried to maintain established surveillance practices by referring to its successful history, especially to its achievements during the Second World War. This positive perception and the emphasis on the risks emanating from cyberspace also strongly resonated in statements delivered by members of the government. The government was quick in stabilising GCHQ's role. Although parliament showed a bit more reluctance in accepting the revealed practices, it also reaffirmed GCHQ's role rather quickly. It was this affirmative interaction that allowed for the stability of British surveillance policies.

Theoretically, the analysis showed that not only historical selves of whole nations shape their foreign policies, but that historical experiences with key agencies also may impact the conduct of foreign policy. Furthermore, the analysis of parliamentary debates illustrated that historical reference points vary, which proposes different roles. This indicates a domestic process of role-making in which government, parliament and others interacted in order to re-evaluate the role of the informant agency. It was the widely shared positive perception of GCHQ that enabled the continuation of surveillance practices.

In the time following the revelations, the government even tried to expand surveillance capabilities. It managed to gain parliamentary support for DRIPA but faced contestation from the High Court of Justice. Nevertheless the Government increased surveillance capabilities even further with the Investigatory Powers Act. Debates about acceptable surveillance policies remain influenced by the positive history of intelligence agencies in the UK. This positive experience also resonated in the public hearings conducted by the ISC in the wake of the Snowden revelations.

What we did at Bletchley Park [...] is rightly regarded as Britain's greatest ever intelligence success. What was that success based on? It was based on the interception of electronically communicated data. The volume may have increased but the principle is still the same. I seriously think we have to give our intelligence and security community the tools it says it needs, and rely that they will deal with it lawfully (Anthony Glees) (ISC 2014: 10).

While reference to positive experiences with intelligence agencies enabled a stabilisation and partly a legalisation of revealed surveillance practices, it remains to be seen whether this reference will also be invoked to expand those capabilities even further.

References

Bakir, V. (2015). "Veillant panoptic assemblage": Mutual watching and resistance to mass surveillance after Snowden. *Media and Communication, 3*(3), 12–25.

Bauman, Z., et al. (2014). After Snowden: Rethinking the impact of surveillance. *International Political Sociology, 8*(2), 121–144.

Blumer, H. (1969). *Symbolic interactionism. Perspective and method.* Englewood Cliffs: Prentice-Hall.

Bochel, H., Defty, A., & Kirkpatrick, J. (2015). 'New mechanisms of independent accountability': Select committees and parliamentary scrutiny of the intelligence services. *Parliamentary Affairs, 68*(2), 314–331.

Boston Consulting Group. (2015). *The internet now contributes 10 percent of GDP to the UK economy, surpassing the manufacturing and retail sectors.* Retrieved April 6, 2016, from http://www.bcg.com/d/press/1may2015-internet-contributes-10-percent-gdp-uk-economy-12111

Brummer, K., & Thies, C. G. (2015). The contested selection of national role conceptions. *Foreign Policy Analysis, 11*(3), 273–293.

Cameron, D. (2013, October). *PM statement on European Council.* Retrieved April 6, 2016, from https://www.gov.uk/government/speeches/pm-statement-on-european-council-october-2013

Cantir, C., & Kaarbo, J. (2012). Contested roles and domestic politics. Reflections on role theory in foreign policy analysis and IR theory. *Foreign Policy Analysis, 8*(1), 5–24.

CJEU. (2014). *The Court of Justice declares the Data Retention Directive to be invalid.* Retrieved April 6, 2016, from http://curia.europa.eu/jcms/upload/docs/application/pdf/2014-04/cp140054en.pdf

Clegg, N. (2014). *Security and privacy in the internet age.* Retrieved April 6, 2016, from https://www.gov.uk/government/speeches/security-and-privacy-in-the-internet-age

Corera, G. (2015). *Intercept: The secret history of computers and spies.* London: Orion.

Davies, P. H. J. (2002). Ideas of intelligence. Divergent national concepts and institutions. *Harvard International Review*, Fall, 62–66.

Davies, P. H. J. (2004). Intelligence culture and intelligence failure in Britain and the United States. *Cambridge Review of International Affairs, 17*(3), 495–520.

DeNardis, L. (2015). The internet design tension between surveillance and security. *IEEE Annals of the History of Computing, 37*(2), 72–83.

Dimmroth, K., & Schünemann, W. J. (2017). The ambiguous relation between privacy and security in German cyber politics. In W. J. Schünemann & M.-B. Baumann (Eds.), *Privacy, data protection and cybersecurity in Europe.* Cham: Springer.

DRIPA. (2014). *Data retention and investigatory powers act 2014.* Retrieved April 6, 2016, from http://www.legislation.gov.uk/ukpga/2014/27/pdfs/ukpga_20140027_en.pdf

EDRi. (2016). *UK's mass surveillance law being rushed through legislative process.* Retrieved April 6, 2016, from https://edri.org/uks-mass-surveillance-law-being-rushed-through-legislative-process/

EP. (2014). *Committee on civil liberties, justice and home affairs.* Report. Retrieved April 6, 2016, from https://polcms.secure.europarl.europa.eu/cmsdata/upload/73108fba-bb11-4a0b-83b8-54cc99c683b5/att_20140306ATT80632-1522917198300865812.pdf

EP. (2015). *European Parliament resolution of 29 October 2015.* Retrieved April 6, 2016, from http://www.europarl.europa.eu/sides/getDoc.do?pubRef=-//EP//NONSGML+TA+P8-TA-2015-0388+0+DOC+PDF+V0//EN

Gibson, S. D. (2009). Future roles of the UK intelligence system. *Review of International Studies, 35*(4), 917–928.

HAC. (2014). *Counter-terrorism seventeenth report of session 2013–14.* Retrieved April 6, 2016, from http://www.publications.parliament.uk/pa/cm201314/cmselect/cmhaff/231/231.pdf

Hague, W. (2013). *Foreign Secretary statement to the House of Commons—GCHQ.* Retrieved April 6, 2016, from https://www.gov.uk/government/speeches/foreign-secretary-statement-to-the-house-of-commons-gchq

Halperin, M. H., Berman, J. J., Borosage, R. L., & Marwick, C. M. (1976). *The lawless state. The crimes of the U.S. intelligence agencies.* Middlesex: Penguin Books.

Hammond, P. (2015). *Foreign Secretary intelligence and security speech.* Retrieved April 6, 2016, from https://www.gov.uk/government/speeches/foreign-secretary-intelligence-and-security-speech

Hannigan, R. (2015). *Keynote speech.* Retrieved April 6, 2016, from https://www.gchq.gov.uk/speech/ia15-robert-hannigans-keynote-speech-delivered

Harnisch, S. (2011). Role theory: Operationalization of key concepts. In S. Harnisch, C. Frank, & H. W. Maull (Eds.), *Role theory in international relations: Approaches and analyses* (pp. 7–15). London: Routledge.

Harnisch, S. (2015). Deutschlands Rolle in der Libyen Intervention: Führung, Gefolgschaft und das angebliche Versagen der Regierung Merkel. In M. Kneuer (Ed.), *Standortbestimmung Deutschlands: Innere Verfasstheit und internationale Verantwortung* (pp. 85–122). Baden-Baden: Nomos.

Harnisch, S. (2016a). Role theory and the study of Chinese foreign policy. In S. Harnisch, S. Bersick, & J.-C. Gottwald (Eds.), *China's international roles: Challenging or supporting international order* (pp. 3–21). New York: Routledge.

Harnisch, S. (2016b). China's historical self and its international role. In S. Harnisch, S. Bersick, & J.-C. Gottwald (Eds.), *China's international roles: Challenging or supporting international order* (pp. 38–58). New York: Routledge.

HCoJ. (2015). *Approved judgment.* Retrieved April 6, 2016, from https://www.judiciary.gov.uk/wp-content/uploads/2015/07/davis_judgment.pdf

HoC. (2013). *Parliamentary Debates—Monday 10 June 2013.* Retrieved April 6, 2016, from http://www.publications.parliament.uk/pa/cm201314/cmhansrd/chan14.pdf

HoC. (2014). *Parliamentary Debates—Tuesday 15 July 2014.* Retrieved April 6, 2016, from http://www.publications.parliament.uk/pa/cm201415/cmhansrd/chan24.pdf

HoC. (2015a). *Parliamentary Debates—Tuesday 24 March 2015.* Retrieved April 6, 2016, from http://www.publications.parliament.uk/pa/cm201415/cmhansrd/chan131.pdf

HoC. (2015b). *Parliamentary Debates—Wednesday 4 November 2015.* Retrieved April 6, 2016, from http://www.publications.parliament.uk/pa/cm201516/cmhansrd/chan64.pdf

HoC. (2016). *Parliamentary Debates—Wednesday 15 March 2016.* Retrieved April 6, 2016, from https://hansard.parliament.uk/pdf/commons/2016-03-15

Holsti, K. J. (1970). National role conceptions in the study of foreign policy. *International Studies Quarterly, 14*(3), 233–309.

IRoTL. (2015). *A question of trust.* Report of the Investigatory Powers Review. Retrieved April 6, 2016, from https://www.gov.uk/government/uploads/system/uploads/attachment_data/file/434399/IPR-Report-Web-Accessible1.pdf

ISC. (2013). *Statement on GCHQ's alleged interception of communications under the US PRISM Programme*. Retrieved April 6, 2016, from https://www.gov.uk/government/uploads/system/uploads/attachment_data/file/225459/ISC-Statement-on-GCHQ.pdf

ISC. (2014). *Privacy and security inquiry. Public evidence session 1*. Retrieved April 6, 2016, from http://isc.independent.gov.uk/public-evidence/14october2014/20141014_ISC_Uncorrected_Tran script_P%2BS_Session1.pdf

ISC. (2015). *Privacy and security: A modern and transparent legal framework*. Retrieved April 6, 2016, from http://isc.independent.gov.uk/files/20150312_ISC_P+S+Rpt(web).pdf

ISC. (2016). *Report on the Draft Investigatory Powers Bill*. Retrieved April 6, 2016, from http://isc.independent.gov.uk/files/20160209_ISC_Rpt_IPBill(web).pdf

JC. (2016). *Draft Investigatory Powers Bill*. Report. Retrieved April 6, 2016, from http://www.publications.parliament.uk/pa/jt201516/jtselect/jtinvpowers/93/93.pdf

Jeffreys-Jones, R. (2013). *In spies we trust: The story of western intelligence*. Oxford: Oxford University Press.

Joergensen, R. F. (2014). Can human rights law bend mass surveillance? *Internet Policy Review, 3*(1).

Kaarbo, J. (2015). A foreign policy analysis perspective on the domestic politics turn in IR theory. *International Studies Review, 17*(2), 189–216.

Kirchner, E. J., & Sperling, J. (Eds.). (2007). *Global threat perception. Elite survey results from Canada, China, the European Union, France, Germany, Italy, Japan, Russia, the United Kingdom and the United States*. Garnet Working Paper 18/07.

Lobban, I. (2013). *Keynote speech at the Defence and Security Dinner*. Retrieved April 6, 2016, from https://www.gchq.gov.uk/speech/director-gchq-gives-keynote-speech-defence-and-secu rity-dinner-6-november-2013

Lobban, I. (2014a). *IA14 closing remarks*. Retrieved April 6, 2016, from https://www.gchq.gov.uk/speech/ia14-director-gchqs-closing-remarks

Lobban, I. (2014b). *Valedictory speech*. Retrieved April 6, 2016, from https://www.gchq.gov.uk/speech/sir-iain-lobbans-valedictory-speech-delivered

Martin, C. (2015). *Speech at infosecurity Europe 2015*. Retrieved April 6, 2016, from https://www.gchq.gov.uk/speech/director-general-cyber-security-speaks-infosecurity-europe-2015

McCourt, D. M. (2012). The roles states play: A Meadian interactionist approach. *Journal of International Relations and Development, 15*(3), 370–392.

Mead, G. H. (1962). *Mind, self, and society. From the standpoint of a social behaviorist*. Chicago: University of Chicago Press.

Moran, C. R. (2013). *Classified. Secrecy and the state in modern Britain*. Cambridge: Cambridge University Press.

Moran, T. H. (2016). *Surveillance versus privacy, with international companies caught in between*. Retrieved April 6, 2016, from http://www.aei.org/wp-content/uploads/2016/03/Sur veillance-versus-privacy.pdf

Ni Loideain, N. (2015). EU law and mass internet metadata surveillance in the Post-Snowden era. *Media and Communication, 3*(2), 53–62.

Open letter. (2014). *An open letter from UK internet law academic experts*. Retrieved April 6, 2016, from http://www.law.ed.ac.uk/__data/assets/pdf_file/0003/158070/Open_letter_UK_internet_law_academics.pdf

OSCE Network. (2014). *Threat perceptions in the OSCE area*. Retrieved April 6, 2016, from http://www.osce.org/networks/118080?download=true

Penney, J. W. (2016). Chilling effects. Online surveillance and Wikipedia use. *Berkeley Technology Law Journal, 31*(1), 118–182.

Phythian, M. (2009). The British intelligence services. In T. Jäger & A. Daun (Eds.), *Geheimdienste in Europa. Transformation, Kooperation und Kontrolle* (pp. 13–34). Wiesbaden: VS Verlag für Sozialwissenschaften.

Sadler, P. (2001). *National security and the D-notice system*. Aldershot: Ashgate.

Schafer, B. (2016). Surveillance for the masses. The political and legal landscape of the UK Investigatory Powers Bill. *Datenschutz und Datensicherheit, 9/2016*, 592–597.

Schulze, M. (2015). Patterns of surveillance legitimization. The German discourse on the NSA scandal. *Surveillance & Society, 13*(2), 197–217.

Snowden, E. (2014). *Interview with the Guardian*. Retrieved April 6, 2016, from http://www.theguardian.com/world/2014/jul/18/-sp-edward-snowden-nsa-whistleblower-interview-transcript

Stahl, T. (2016). Indiscriminate mass surveillance and the public sphere. *Ethics and Information Technology, 18*, 33–39.

STC. (2016). *Investigatory Powers Bill. Technology issues*. Retrieved April 6, 2016, from http://www.publications.parliament.uk/pa/cm201516/cmselect/cmsctech/573/573.pdf

The Guardian. (2013). *NSA files: Why the Guardian in London destroyed hard drives of leaked files*. Retrieved April 6, 2016, from http://www.theguardian.com/world/2013/aug/20/nsa-snowden-files-drives-destroyed-london

The Guardian. (2014). *ISPs take GCHQ to court in UK over mass surveillance*. Retrieved April 6, 2016, from http://www.theguardian.com/world/2014/jul/02/isp-gchq-mass-surveillance-privacy-court-claim

The Guardian. (2015). *The spooks have come out of the shadows—for now*. Retrieved April 6, 2016, from http://www.theguardian.com/uk-news/2015/oct/28/snowden-surveillance-and-public-relations

Thies, C. (2013). *The United States, Israel, and the search for international order: Socializing states*. New York: Routledge.

Thomas, R. M. (1991). *Espionage and secrecy. The official secrets acts 1911–1989 of the United Kingdom*. London: Routledge.

UN. (2016). *Report of the Special Rapporteur on the right to privacy*. Retrieved April 6, 2016, from http://www.ohchr.org/Documents/Issues/Privacy/A-HRC-31-64.doc

Wehner, L. E., & Thies, C. G. (2014). Role theory, narratives, and interpretation: The domestic contestation of roles. *International Studies Review, 16*(3), 411–436.

The Ambiguous Relation Between Privacy and Security in German Cyber Politics

A Discourse Analysis of Governmental and Parliamentary Debates

Katharina Dimmroth and Wolf J. Schünemann

1 Introduction: The Endangered Balance Between Privacy and Security After Snowden

As argued at greater length in the introductory chapter of this volume, recent events in the related fields of cybersecurity and data protection have renewed debates over the old and constantly endangered relationship between the fundamental values of freedom and security. Both values, as well as the tension between them, need to be re-investigated in the digital age. The Snowden revelations have given a clearer picture of the relative power of security actors who use technology for sophisticated surveillance on the one hand and advocates of personal freedom on the other hand. Debates on cybersecurity and privacy or data protection thus increasingly collide. Therefore, it is understandably far from easy to disentangle notions of privacy and cybersecurity when looking at social and political reactions to the revelations. However, it is important to do so if one wishes to differentiate between the two phenomena, their perceptions and the fields of action they give rise to. The main aim of this chapter is to analyse the German governmental and parliamentary discourses on cybersecurity in order to differentiate patterns of communication that belong to the field of cybersecurity and those that instead have to do with data protection. We analyse and reconstruct problem definitions and independently made political solutions, but also the common conceptual grounds and the ways in which speakers relate them to each other.

K. Dimmroth
RWTH Aachen University, Aachen, Germany

W.J. Schünemann (✉)
Hildesheim University, Hildesheim, Germany
e-mail: wolf.schuenemann@uni-hildesheim.de

© Springer International Publishing AG 2017
W.J. Schünemann, M.-O. Baumann (eds.), *Privacy, Data Protection and Cybersecurity in Europe*, DOI 10.1007/978-3-319-53634-7_7

2   The Discourse Analytical Approach

In the last decade, discourse analysis (DA) has been increasingly embraced by mainstream political science, as many researchers apply DA methods in studying their subjects. This holds true even for the fields of International Relations and Security Studies (Herschinger and Renner 2014), where researchers seemed to be more hesitant towards a post-modernist understanding of discourse, not least because the Habermasian idea of discourse had gained ground in IR much earlier (Habermas 1984, 1996). With the post-modernist tradition as common ground, however, empirical discourse researchers entered a new area of social science research, wherein many different paths had been developed beforehand (for an overview see Diaz-Bone et al. 2007).

Discourse analysis also looms large as the methodological orientation of many researchers in the field of cybersecurity. A high number of scholars consistently apply a securitisation theory or logic (Buzan et al. 1998; Balzacq 2011) to the political measures for securing cyberspace across the world. Often, these applications are combined with some kind of discourse analytical method (Dunn Cavelty 2014; Gartzke 2013; Gorr and Schünemann 2013; Guitton 2013; Hansen and Nissenbaum 2009). While securitisation-inspired works tend to critically reflect on how so-called securitising actors succeed in making an issue a security concern and thus legitimise extraordinary measures and competences, our perspective is the clear opposite. We look at how extraordinary practices—at least those depicted in public discourse as such—have been revealed, then discussed, questioned and potentially challenged by political actors on different stages.

Given the different strands of discourse-related works, it is no wonder that new discourse researchers are confronted with a plethora of different DA approaches that vary widely in their terminology and methodology. Despite the variety, there are some core decisions every DA must make. First, it has to define the object. What is the discourse and how does it relate to non-discursive events and the practices of social actors? Second, it needs to be clear about the material that is to be studied. Researchers should build a balanced corpus for their field of study. Third, it should be pre-defined how the elements in the corpus are to be systematically analysed. The abstract interpretive analytics should be outlined clearly before the research begins. This does not include—of course—the definition of concrete categories. Instead, discourse analysis is open to any kind of inductive research practice. In our project, for instance, we apply a Grounded-Theory-Methodology (GTM; Glaser et al. 2010).

But let us go one by one through the decisions we have made for this study. Being interested in how socio-historically specific knowledge is constructed, formed and processed through time, how it is materially manifested in social communication and how this discourse exerts power on individual actors as it structures and restricts what can be said and thought in a given situation, we selected the Foucauldian discourse theory (Foucault 2002) for our study. In order to make Foucauldian discourse theory more applicable to the phenomena at hand and provide more guidance for concrete social science research, we also chose the Sociology of Knowledge Approach to Discourse (SKAD), developed by German sociologist Reiner Keller in the late 1990s (Keller 2008, 2013). One of the main advantages of SKAD is that in contrast to the Foucauldian work, where it originates, it brings the social actor back into focus. Following a pragmatist tradition with the sociology of knowledge (Berger and Luckmann 1969), the social actor is not just conceived of as a materialisation machine for predetermined statements but as an actor who brings meaning to his/her world through interpretation. The knowledge and categories needed for understanding and interpreting the world are received through socialisation. Social knowledge is conserved, processed and transformed in discourses. This is where the two strands (Foucauldian discourse theory and sociology of knowledge) converge in SKAD. For our study, we are interested in two kinds of special discourses, namely parliamentary debates on the one hand and various speeches and statements made by government officials, belonging to the relevant policy subsystem (here: the security and intelligence field), on the other.

Having said that, it is clear which sorts of documents we sought to include in our data selection and corpus building. Given our interest in the development of discourses after the Snowden revelations, we can define temporal criteria for data selection in addition to the institutional setting of the debate or the affiliation of the speaker. We were interested in these discourses from June 2013 up to May 2015. While for the parliamentary discourse we mostly relied on minutes of the plenary debates, data selection for governmental discourse was done in an actor-centred way (see below).

Thirdly, a weakness of many discourse analytical studies is transparency regarding the interpretive work. Approaches that give clear guidance on how to perform the empirical research—from the first coding via interpretation to the integration of results—are very rare. While SKAD also is not perfect in this regard, it nevertheless provides the analyst with a research framework encompassing a set of basic analytical tools and concepts. First of all, discourses are analysed by dissecting recurrent statements. For a deeper analysis of the statements, SKAD proposes a set of interpretive schemes, including several sub-types such as frames, narratives, classifications and phenomenal structures (Keller 2008: 240–249). Frames are for examining how social actors regularly make sense of the developments they observe by discussing and regulating as political actors. In our example, a very basic frame is whether actors perceive and depict the revealed practices of mass surveillance as a fundamental breach of privacy rights or an acceptable collateral effect of the intelligence gathering necessary for the security of the people. An example of the narrative subcategory might be the story of US intelligence services getting out of control after having gained more authority following the terrorist attacks of 2001. Another recurrent story would be the German dictatorial regimes that widely misused their secret services for the suppression of people in the past.

3   Case Selection and Corpus-Building

Germany, in comparison to other European nations, was for a number of reasons the country where public anger about the revealed practices of mass surveillance seemed highest and where the subsequent political debate received the most attention from national and international media. This is related to the fact that Germany is, in international terms, traditionally very sensitive to data protection issues. Furthermore, in the early phase after the revelations, there was a general election campaign going on in Germany, which channelled much attention to the NSA scandal and the unrealistic promise of reaching a no-spy agreement with the US. Attention did not waver after the elections, as in October 2013 newly revealed documents showed that Merkel's smartphone had also been targeted by foreign surveillance. While the reactions in other countries were of a much lesser intensity, some being rather oriented towards the German debate (see Weiland 2017), it should be evident that Germany occupied the role of the irritated ally potentially betrayed by its main partner, the US. As public outrage and attention were extremely high (whereas the outcomes in terms of reform were little, see Steiger et al. forthcoming), Germany is a very good case for studying parliamentary and governmental discourses after the Snowden revelations.

As to data collection, we combined an actor-centred approach for governmental actors (websites of governmental actors and agencies) and an institution-centred approach for the parliament (minutes of the plenary debates). Both types of sources were queried with the same query terms in the same period of time (the 2 years after the Snowden revelations, i.e. 1 June 2013–31 May 2015). The texts were compiled using specific query terms. These were intuitively selected and then validated and expanded using the "relative query term relevance" (RQTR) method proposed by Costas Gabrielatos (2007). We started with the German terms *Cyberangriff* ("cyberattack") and *Cybersicherheit* ("cybersecurity"). After the RQTR test, we added "CERT" (Cyber Emergency Response Team) and "Stuxnet"[1] as query terms. Our resulting corpus includes 161 documents in total, 119 coming from governmental websites and 42 being extracts from minutes of plenary debates in the German Bundestag.

4   Comparing Problem Definitions: Interpretive Schemes on What It Is All About

Political speech and action are problem-oriented. Thus, reconstruction of the problem definition as the most basic element in the political creation of meaning is a fundamental step in any political discourse analysis. This basic operation is

---

[1] Stuxnet is the name of a very sophisticated malware (worm) that was detected in 2010. The worm infected systems across the world but had Iraninan facilities for the enrichment of Uranium as prime target. The attribution shared by many experts is to the US and Israel.

done in the following section. For both overarching concepts, data protection and cybersecurity, we identify the most important and competing frames regarding the problem or issue itself. Political speech and action are of course not only problem- but also solution-oriented (see also Tiainen 2017). From this perspective, as politics is about the design of the future, problem definition can be regarded as a preparatory step for subsequent proposals for political action that are made in reaction to the problem or challenge identified. In the proposed actions, the same or related frames and other interpretive schemes should be present. Finally, problem definition and the range of possible solutions are more fundamentally structured by a meta- understanding of cyberspace, the digitised world or the internet. Importantly, this meta-understanding seems to be embedded in a more fundamental narrative widely shared among political actors and the public. This has been revealed and discussed by many cybersecurity scholars already, but it is also relevant for discourses on privacy. This meta-narrative is the story of cyberspace having developed into a more and more dangerous place where users, firms, states and other social entities risk being endangered or harmed. It produces an increased level of threat percep- tion, or what Singer and Friedman (2014: 3) call "cyber anxiety". Before we turn to problem-definition and solutions made in the two fields, we present illustrations of this more fundamental interpretive scheme in the following subsection.

4.1   Increased Level of Threat Perception: Cyber Anxiety

The story of cyberspace as a dangerous place is a narrative prevalent in both parliamentary and governmental discourse that sets the tone for problem defini- tions, assumptions and propositions in these fields. In more nuanced terms, this is the narrative that digitisation has brought about new threats for individuals but also firms, states and its citizens' security. One telling example is the following state- ment made by the social democrat Hakverdi:

> Today one is able to launch an attack from afar at any point, from any place in the world (. . .) Today it's about professional criminal structures or even intelligence agencies who have even more resources (Metin Hakverdi, Deutscher Bundestag 2015).

The speakers employing this narrative portray these cyber threats as innovative, ubiquitous, invisible, scalable and constant. Relentless attacks are said to take place on a daily basis, and no user can be secure. For internet users, this narrative has the potential to produce a diffuse feeling of insecurity when communicating online or making any kind of transaction via the internet. Thus, the feeling of cyber anxiety comes closest to what has been described at length in the cyber-related securitisation literature (Guitton 2013; Hansen and Nissenbaum 2009). We label the narrative in accordance with cybersecurity scholars Singer and Friedman (2014: 3) as "cyber anxiety". In the meta-narrative, the perpetrators remain diffuse. On the one hand, it would be easy to see that all kind of criminal activities profit from the use of widely spread, often insufficiently protected computer networks for handling trustworthy information or even making economic transactions. So indeed, there are criminals online, but this is not all that makes up the threat perception. Moreover, there are cyberwarriors and terrorists who could potentially attack the critical infrastructures of society and even cause material damage remotely. From this perspective, cyber threats are not just an issue for police work and homeland affairs—they can also represent grave challenges of international politics, security and order, as the following statement by Markus Ederer, state secretary in the Foreign Ministry, clearly shows:

> Numerous states are pursuing military cyber-capabilities. However, traditional political-military strategies are difficult to adjust to the cyber-space. During the Cold War, the opposing parties relied on defence efforts as well as arms control and confidence building measures. Such defensive approaches require that the consequences of any attack be clearly and credibly communicated ex ante to any potential adversary. This can be difficult in cyber-space, where you often have to guess who the adversary is. Uncertainty about the origin of hostile cyber-action is a characteristic of cyber-incidents. As a consequence, the masters of cyber capabilities favour the offense. This introduces an element of dangerous instability into international affairs (Ederer 2014).

In this quote, we find that the increased level of threat perception is not only due to the fact that cyberspace offers yet another means of attacking a state and its citizens; it also describes how this new means influences 'regular' international affairs between states as they develop offensive instead of defensive strategies to ward off potential threats. The Commissioner of cyber foreign affairs, Riedel, even uses the Cold War to exemplify former defensive efforts, implicitly positioning the cyber age as an entirely new era for international relations:

> One state has a tense relationship to its neighbour maybe because of a border dispute. Suddenly a cyber-attack happens and all communications services are disrupted. Telephones no longer work and nobody is able to access the internet. The situation worsens; other sectors are affected, such as the power grid or the banking system. It might have been an individual who planted this virus, but suspicions run high that the less friendly neighbour perpetrated a cyber-attack. How to respond? Is this a case where the attacked state may use its right to self-defence? The danger of escalation is evident (Riedel 2015).

As the Commissioner states in this quote, the anonymity of cyberattacks is inherently dangerous, as these threats can be attributed to any actor that enjoys a less than favourable relationship with the victim of the attack. It is therefore up to the actor suffering the attack to decide on a course of action against whatever party they believe to be responsible, the most extreme case being an offensive self-defence effort against an enemy state.

Finally—and this is what Snowden essentially revealed—there is surveillance going on in cyberspace, surveillance of the governmental, but also of the corporate sort. This surveillance is carried out for security reasons, for economic gain or some mixture of the two, as foreign intelligence agencies are accused of having conducted business espionage. Thus, the meta-narrative of cyberspace as a dangerous place and 'cyber anxiety' as an abstract result are diffuse in concept and, what is more, in their implications. For on the one hand, criminal activity such as data theft, ransomware or even terrorism emphasizes the need for increased cybersecurity. On the other hand, governments seeking to bolster security intrude on the privacy of their own as well as foreign citizens and help make the case for increased data protection (Nissenbaum 2005).

While the former observations are quite in line with what securitisation scholars would tell us, there are more nuanced instances of the same argument as well.

> Nevertheless, an all-out 'cyber war' seems unlikely at present. In fact, the term 'cyber war' is inadequate and misleading. It implies an extensive, existential threat to a state solely through targeted attacks by other states on computer systems and IT networks, or through other actions in cyberspace. This seems unrealistic for the foreseeable future (Riedel 2015).

This statement is especially interesting, considering that it doesn't deny the existence of cyber threats but rather aims to assure the reader that these threats do not rise to an existential level as they seem to in the cyber anxiety meta-narrative. The idea of a state being attacked solely via cyber means by another state is deemed 'unrealistic'; the importance and the level of threat is being downplayed. These opposite interpretive schemes once again strike at the heart of the post-Snowden discourse by invoking the tension between personal freedom and security.

4.2 Data Protection

Data protection as a concern for political action has a long tradition, at least in Germany and other European states. However, the problem definition has changed, mostly due to the effects of digitisation.

> On the one hand, there is fear of the omnipotent state. The fear that the age of Big Data is turning into an age of Big Brother. (...) But on the other hand, I also sense in the public the opposite fear: a fear of the impotent state. People are worried that Big Brother lurks when they search for a restaurant or order a book online (Steinmeier 2014a).

We find that the problem of securing data is twofold in the digital age. Both governmental (whether foreign or not) and economic actors are seeking to attain data from citizens, leaving the citizens with a general sense of unease about their privacy online. There are two fundamental and partially competing approaches to the issue. The basic question to answer is whose responsibility it is to safeguard the informational privacy of the individual user. One of the basic frames we identified defines the responsibility as laying with the users or citizens themselves.

> We shouldn't pretend that a citizen is safe from espionage if they expose themselves by disclosing private material on the internet. (...) We have to tell them that what they put online stays online and that there's no digital eraser. That's an illusion. We have to tell people that (Hans-Peter Uhl, Deutscher Bundestag 2013a).

By advocating this type of self-responsibility, the speakers (here a Christian Democrat) absolve the government of blame for the intrusion of privacy that the NSA affair brought to light. It further establishes that data protection is to an extent a private matter, as citizens should expect their data to be exploited once it is put online. The answer is thus data parsimony or data self-protection. The responsibility of the state, then, is merely to inform citizens of this situation and increase their risk awareness, to help them make their own informed choices regarding the handling of their personal data.

The opposite view on this matter is that protecting citizens' data is the task of the state and that further political action is necessary to get it achieved. This more consumer-protection oriented argument turns up far more often in parliamentary than in governmental discourse, as made in the following quote by the chairman of the NSA investigation committee at the German Bundestag:

> These are our tasks. This is the only way we'll be able to regain trust, which is necessary for the citizens in our country to be certain that the parliament and this government are doing everything possible to safeguard online communication [...] (Clemens Binninger, Deutscher Bundestag 2014).

The NSA affair revealed the woeful scarcity of data protection provided to German citizens by their government. Therefore, it is not surprising to find that the argument espousing citizen protection as a task of the nation state is much less prevalent in governmental discourse than it is in parliamentary discourse.

> Here is what I think: I think the state has an important role to play in internet governance. But it can only do so if it builds trust. Trust with all the stakeholders I have been describing: its own citizens, international partners, businesses, users (Steinmeier 2014a).

Even in this instance, the responsibility of the state is only implicitly referred to as 'having a role to play' in internet governance. The unequivocal demand to put the responsibility of data protection on the state, as we identified it in the parliamentary argument of citizen protection, is lacking in the governmental documents.

A very clear assessment was given by Interior Minister de Maizière, expressing the opinion that data protection is a task citizens must perform for themselves:

> The use of personal freedom is ultimately part of being a responsible citizen and not an area in need of regulation by politicians (de Maizière 2014).

The idea that the state has a responsibility to ensure personal freedom by providing data protection is firmly rejected by the Minister in this statement. Instead, he propagates the idea that part of being a responsible citizen is the safeguarding of one's own personal freedom.

However, as other actors, including governmental ones, indeed do acknowledge the role of the state in data protection, it is worth looking at which more concrete solutions for regulation are presented, including the protection of communications from foreign surveillance. Concrete propositions are made that outline possible means of improving data protection.

One of these is to strengthen the European Union and develop policy guidelines on data protection at the supranational level. Although it is suited to shift the burden at least partly from the national government to the supranational level, the argument is even made by the Green opposition politician Ströbele:

> What we have here is a European problem. All of Europe, its peoples and parliaments feel threatened by the NSA, which extracts, analyses and saves the data of Europe's citizens,

either from the US or even here. This is a European problem and it demands a European solution (Hans-Christian Ströbele, Deutscher Bundestag 2014).

This argument is common in parliamentary and governmental discourse, which can be partly explained by the fact that the EU General Data Protection Regulation, adopted only in 2016, was being worked on during the span of time studied in this chapter. Given its supranational quality and its international effects, it is depicted as one of the possible solutions to the issue raised by the Snowden revelations:

> I hope that by the end of the year the proceedings will be finalised and that we'll then have a General Data Protection Regulation in the European Union that will provide more data protection on a European level and more security in the digital age (de Maizière 2015).

This argument advocates for taking the issue of data protection to a supranational level and using a regulatory framework to protect every EU citizen's data. Though on the supranational level, the proposition is in accordance with other arguments, which orient towards territorial forms of internet regulation.

4.3 Cybersecurity

The need for cybersecurity and the state's involvement in it is often expressed using the narrative of the endangered critical infrastructures, which, if accepted, understandably moves the level of threat perception much higher than if it is 'only' about malware and damaged computer systems or networks. Sketching a vision of the most devastating potential consequence of cyberattacks, the story is often told that critical infrastructures, such as communication networks, hospitals or power plants, may be targeted by a cyberattack and partly destroyed:

> The dependence of the modern world on the Internet also means that cyber incidents can escalate into 'real-life' conflict or even war. (. . .) All of a sudden, the main telephone and internet provider becomes victim to a software bug. Nobody can make phone calls, there are no e-mails. Government, banks, security services are paralyzed. Critical infrastructure is affected. The damage is enormous. (. . .) Suspicions run high that the less friendly neighbour perpetrated a cyber-attack. How to respond? The danger of escalation is evident (Ederer 2014).

The basic line of this narrative is that as technology advances more and more, the basic infrastructural needs of a modern society grow more dependent on networked computer systems. Attacking these networks could have widespread consequences with devastating effects that endanger the functioning of our society and even the lives of citizens. Therefore, the industries using this type of technology are in need of protection from the state:

> Therefore, it is right that the government has declared its intention of introducing an IT security bill. We have to ensure that our critical infrastructure is being effectively safeguarded (Stephan Mayer, Deutscher Bundestag 2014).

The focus on a European solution is thus not just part of the discourse dealing with data protection. Regarding cybersecurity, the parliamentary discourse includes an argumentation that postulates a European or wider multilateral framework for strengthening cybersecurity. Conventions of the Council of Europe or the draft of an EU Directive on Security of Network and Information Systems (NIS) are important documents for reference in this area (see also Jasmontaite and Pavel Burloiu 2017). Beyond that, transatlantic relations are of course mentioned as well:

> The internet is a global good. It has always crossed borders. And for us to keep it that way, our foreign policy has to react, especially our transatlantic policy (Steinmeier 2014b).

The need for a solution that crosses national borders leads to the relational dimension under critique after the Snowden revelations. When it comes to security and intelligence cooperation with the US as a fundamental means to guarantee (cyber) security, we find one of the most obvious differences between parliamentary and governmental discourses in the number of times the Snowden revelations are brought up by the speakers. This can be shown by a mere relative word count: governmental speakers refer to Snowden less than half as often as their colleagues in parliament. Given the fact that the government became the target of criticism due to the Snowden revelations, this is not very surprising. The mentions we do find tend to put the revelations into their own perspective by justifying the intelligence cooperation with the United States, as Interior Minister Friedrich does so in the following statement:

> We expect further clarification. But it's also true that the Americans are essential partners to us in the area of terror prevention. We exchange important information (Friedrich 2013).

In contrast to the emphasis put on international relations and cooperation, there are indications for a growing sense of so-called digital sovereignty, at least in German parliamentary discourse post-Snowden. Speakers are concerned about the protection of German firms against industrial espionage. The arguments thus evolve around Germany's economic interests and the protection of national industries. From this perspective, the proposed measures are not only defensive or protective, but even suited to secure economic gains—national industries stand to lose billions by being the target of foreign espionage, as social democrat Oppermann argues:

> Our corporations are suffering billion dollar losses through economic espionage. We can't protect them from it effectively enough. That's why we have to think about the recovery or at least partial restoration of our technological sovereignty. That means safe networks, secure communication, encryption and further preventive measures. (...) The NSA affair has to be a wake-up call for all of us (Thomas Oppermann, Deutscher Bundestag 2013b).

In this instance the Snowden revelations are being used to underscore the negative consequences of weak protections for German industries and corporations. The NSA affair is used to argue the interests of national industries rather than that of private citizens.

5   The Ambiguous Relation Disentangled: Normative Assessments by Governmental and Parliamentary Speakers

5.1   Towards a Balance of Privacy and (Cyber-)Security

After having looked at discourses on data protection and cybersecurity separately, our second step is to discuss sequences, wherein speakers explicitly set the two competing goals in relation to each other: thus privacy or data protection on the one hand and (cyber-)security on the other. All in all, we found that attempts for comparative assessment appear more often in parliamentary than in governmental discourse, which might indicate the more intense discussion on the fundamental problem revealed by Edward Snowden.

> You keep telling us that freedom and security belong together and that freedom isn't possible without security. (...) We know there is a balance to be struck in this tense relationship. But we arrive at very different conclusions as to how this balance ought to look (Renate Künast, Deutscher Bundestag 2013a).

Even as the speaker acknowledges the general consensus reached by governmental and parliamentary actors on the need for a balance between cybersecurity and data protection, she nevertheless accuses the government (in this particular case Interior Minister Friedrich) of having fundamentally different ideas on how this balance ought to be achieved. The perception of the problem is congruent even as the solution completely differs.

However, at least when speaking before parliament, governmental speakers give their reflections on the fundamental dilemma as well, as the following quote of Interior Minister Friedrich illustrates:

> We always have to make sure—this is what I believe the Chancellor said during her visit with the US President—that the cooperation between intelligence agencies is done according to law and especially within reason. This means that the goal we want to reach—security—has to be reconcilable with the intrusion on privacy. We have to find the proper balance (Dr. Hans-Peter Friedrich, Deutscher Bundestag 2013a).

The "balance" that Friedrich speaks of is frequently invoked by speakers of all parties in parliament and governmental actors as well. This initial concession that there are two overarching goals that need to be balanced has practically become a standard discursive element and seems to be the common ground for all actors in the German post-Snowden debate. Put differently, ignoring that there is a problem at all, as we have partly seen in the British post-Snowden debate (see Steiger 2017), seems to be considered as being beyond the sayable and is thus not an option for political actors in Germany. The following quote by Friedrich's successor, Interior Minister de Maizière, is telling in this regard. What starts as a clear and personal commitment to privacy rights ends as a clarification and redefinition of the concept, as it is said not to be equal with anonymity in online communication:

> The central question is how to find a balance between personhood and anonymity. I won't give up the struggle for continued personal privacy. To anyone who thinks that to be outdated I say: personal privacy is more important in the digital age than ever. But at the same time we cannot confuse personal privacy with anonymity. Personhood, responsibility and liability for one's actions are a central part of our legal culture (Dr. Thomas de Maizière 2014).

Instead of a principled commitment to privacy, we see a qualified one. The qualifier used in this example is that anonymity cannot be the end goal when taking the need for personal privacy into account, as it would collide with the interest of security actors in identifying every user on the internet if necessary.

Thus, while many speakers refer to the concept of a dilemma or at least concede that two goals need to be balanced some way, discursive differences become obvious on a deeper level of analysis. As we will see in the next two subsections, in many instances we observe a hierarchy of the leading goals. Either privacy is given precedence over (cyber-)security needs or (cyber-)security is depicted as the transcendental good without which everything else is meaningless.

5.2 Privacy as the Transcendental Good: Informational Self-Determination

The frame which sees privacy as the transcendental good appears often and dominates only in parliamentary discourse. We found far fewer examples in governmental discourse. This is congruent with our assumption that speakers in parliament will come down more firmly on the side of privacy and data protection, as they include the opposition and are generally more critical of the German government's cybersecurity cooperation with the United States in intelligence matters.

> The end does not justify the means, not even in the fight against terrorism. Our answer to the threat of international terrorism, which indeed exists, has to be: more freedom, a stronger state of law, more democracy. That especially means the defence and recapture of free communication (. . .) (Jan Korte, Deutscher Bundestag 2015).

This instance shows how fundamentally speakers in parliament (here from the leftist opposition party) disagree with the government course on fighting terrorism. The battle cry of 'more security' is being offset by the demand for more freedom, which so often is being quoted by governmental actors as allowing terrorists to thrive. Once again, we find that the problem definition is very similar, whether it is employed by governmental or parliamentary speakers. The difference lies in the solutions these actors propose, with the parliament more often coming down on the side of freedom than their governmental colleagues.

> The protection of privacy is determined by the basic rights of our constitution. Therefore, the 'glass citizen' isn't reconcilable with our state's understanding of the constitution. The state's actions, the actions of all governmental agencies—and that includes security

agencies and intelligence agencies—have to be carried out according to law (Dr. Hans-Peter Friedrich, Deutscher Bundestag 2013a).

Here, Friedrich argues that it is parliament's task to oversee governmental action and ensure that citizens' rights are not being violated. There is a tendency to emphasise the aspects wherein both goals coincide, for example the security of personal data against breaches and theft.

> In a global, interconnected world, protection against cyberattacks such as the theft of online identities plays a much bigger role. Personal privacy and individual freedom on the internet are goods that need to be protected (Bundesregierung 2014).

The above quote clearly states the importance of privacy and the protection of personal data and how its importance has increased in the digital age when so much information about a person is readily available online. The protection of privacy here is fully in line with cybersecurity needs, as identity theft online clearly belongs to the classical IT security goals (confidentiality, integrity, availability). To put it differently: instead of putting both goals in opposition to each other, they are depicted as interconnected principles, whereby cybersecurity (here in the narrower sense of data security) serves privacy goals.

5.3   (Cyber)Security as the Transcendental Good

Given our expectations and the results presented before, we were surprised to find that the '(cyber)security as transcendental good' assessment is not used significantly more often in governmental discourse than in parliamentary discourse. Perhaps even more surprising, it seems to be even less important to governmental than to parliamentary discourse post-Snowden. We found few instances wherein any ordering of priorities came out particularly clearly at all:

> Security is prerequisite to freedom (Hans-Dieter Heumann, Bundesakademie für Sicherheitspolitik 2015).

A similar statement came with the frequently cited reaction of Interior Minister Friedrich, who coined the concept of "Supergrundrecht Sicherheit" (supreme fundamental right, Bewarder and Jungholt, welt.de 2013) in his early response to the Snowden revelations. One possible explanation for the surprising rarity of such statements is that the government attempted to draw as little attention as possible to cybersecurity and intelligence cooperation with the United States at that time, especially not to its own involvement in the revealed surveillance practices.

Looking at the Bundestag again, the picture is not as different as expected. True, principled commitments to privacy and data protection are dominant in parliamentary discourse, but we also found a number of instances wherein speakers allocate the utmost importance to cybersecurity and the need to further it by allowing intelligence agencies a certain leniency.

> We can only effectively react to terrorist structures and certain types of organised crime if we attain information about those networks and then prevent attacks and destroy those networks (Dr. Günter Krings, Deutscher Bundestag 2013b).

The underlying interpretive scheme supports the idea that cybersecurity is a transcendental good that has to take precedence over personal freedom. Therefore, intelligence agencies must be allowed certain liberties to ensure that terrorist and criminal networks are not able to thrive by using the relative anonymity of the internet to organise. The privacy of the average citizen must endure scrutiny to ensure their physical safety.

6   Conclusion

In this chapter, we set out to explore German discourse on cybersecurity and data protection in the wake of the Snowden revelations. His disclosure of the mass surveillance being employed by US intelligence agencies invoked outrage and triggered a debate on the extent to which states should curtail freedom for the sake of achieving security, especially in the digital age. Germany, being an important target of NSA surveillance as well as a state with a long and difficult history of privacy intrusions and their devastating consequences, was especially scrutinised once Snowden's claims became public. Our goal was to analyse German governmental and parliamentary discourse in the two years after the Snowden revelations and to somewhat disentangle the notions of cybersecurity and data protection, which often get thrown into the same category. In order to achieve this, we gathered documents originating from the German parliament and government and analysed them using the Sociology of Knowledge Approach to Discourse (SKAD), which allows for an actor-focused approach within discourse analysis. One of our main findings was that both discourses contained an extremely prevalent meta-narrative of *cyber anxiety* that credits the digital age with bringing about many new threats by allowing criminals and terrorists to use the internet for nefarious purposes and letting both corporate entities and governments attack citizens' privacy by collecting and analysing personal data. Against the backdrop of this meta-narrative, we sought to identify problem definitions as well as proposed solutions in the discursive area of cybersecurity and data protection in the first two sections of our empirical analysis. The final section dealt with frames and narratives that set these issues in relation to one another. Overall, we attempted to identify differences in how governmental speakers employed these frames and narratives in comparison to politicians in parliament. Our assumption that parliamentary speakers more prevalently use frames and narratives that prioritise privacy and personal freedom over the need for cybersecurity was confirmed by the results of the analysis. Especially when talking about possible solutions to the identified problems, parliamentary speakers spoke out more firmly on the need for data protection and privacy. One of the surprises in our results was the disputation of our assumption that the issue of (cyber)security and especially the framing of this issue as an overarching, transcendental good did not turn out to be considerably prevalent in governmental discourse. Considering that governmental speakers were in the position of having to defend the German security cooperation with the United States, we expected there to be more instances in which the importance of cybersecurity was underscored than we actually found. One possible explanation is that governmental speakers were so reluctant to discuss anything relating to their own involvement in the NSA affair that they simply did not dare to put too much emphasis on the security issue at all.

References

Balzacq, T. (2011). A theory of securitization. Origins, core assumptions, and variants. In T. Balzacq (Ed.), *PRIO new security studies. Securitization theory. How security problems emerge and dissolve* (pp. 1–30). London: Routledge.

Berger, P. L., & Luckmann, T. (1969). *Die gesellschaftliche Konstruktion der Wirklichkeit. Eine Theorie der Wissenssoziologie.* Frankfurt: Fischer.

Bewarder, M., & Jungholt, T., welt.de. (2013). *Friedrich erklärt Sicherheit zum "Supergrundrecht".* Retrieved December 12, 2016, from https://www.welt.de/politik/deutsch land/article118110002/Friedrich-erklaert-Sicherheit-zum-Supergrundrecht.html

Bundesakademie für Sicherheitspolitik. (2015). *Cyber-Realität zwischen Freiheit und Sicherheit.* https://www.baks.bund.de/de/aktuelles/cyber-realitaet-zwischen-freiheit-und-sicherheit

Bundesregierung. (2014). *Neue Hightech-Strategie—Innovationen für Deutschland.* Online verfügbar unter: https://www.bmbf.de/pub_hts/HTS_Broschure_Web.pdf

Buzan, B., Waever, O., & de Wilde, J. (1998). *Security: A new framework for analysis.* Boulder: Lynne Rienner.

de Maizière, T. (2014, June 23). *Rede des Bundesministers des Innern bei der Konferenz für Datenschutz und Datensicherheit (DuD).*

de Maizière, T. (2015, May 23). *Rede des Bundesministers des Innern zum Entwurf des IT-Sicherheitsgesetzes, Berlin.*

Deutscher Bundestag. (2013a, June 26). *Plenarprotokoll. Stenografischer Bericht der 249. Sitzung der 17. Wahlperiode.*

Deutscher Bundestag. (2013b, November 18). *Stenografischer Bericht der 2. Sitzung der 18. Wahlperiode, Berlin.*

Deutscher Bundestag. (2014, January 15). *Plenarprotokoll. Stenografischer Bericht der 7. Sitzung der 18 Wahlperiode.*

Deutscher Bundestag. (2015, June 12). *Plenarprotokoll. Stenografischer Bericht der 110. Sitzung der 18. Wahlperiode.*

Diaz-Bone, R., Bührmann, A. D., Rodríguez, E. G., Schneider, W., Kendall, G., & Tirado, F. (2007). The field of Foucaultian discourse analysis. *Forum: Qualitative Social Research (FQS)* (No. 2, Art. 30), 8.

Dunn Cavelty, M. (2014). Breaking the cyber-security dilemma: Aligning security needs and removing vulnerabilities. *Science and Engineering Ethics, 20*(3), 701–715. doi:10.1007/s11948-014-9551-y.

Ederer, M. (2014, December 4). *Rede von Staatssekretär Markus Ederer beim Cyber Cooperation Summit.*

Foucault, M. (2002). *Archaeology of knowledge. Routledge classics.* London: Routledge.

Friedrich, H.-P. (2013, November 30). *Diese Daten helfen uns. Interview mit Bundesinnenminister Dr. Hans-Peter Friedrich.*

Gabrielatos, C. (2007). Selecting query terms to build a specialized corpus from a restricted-access database. *ICAME Journal, 31*, 5–43.

Gartzke, E. (2013). The myth of cyberwar: Bringing war in cyberspace back down to earth. *International Security, 38*(2), 41–73. doi:10.1162/ISEC_a_00136.

Glaser, B. G., Strauss, A. L., & Paul, A. T. (2010). *Grounded theory: Strategien qualitativer Forschung. Programmbereich Gesundheit* (3rd ed.). Bern: Huber.

Gorr, D., & Schünemann, W. J. (2013). Creating a secure cyberspace: Securitization in Internet governance discourses and dispositives in Germany and Russia. *International Review of Information Ethics, 20*(12), 37–51. http://www.i-r-i-e.net/inhalt/020/IRIE-Gorr-Schuenemann.pdf

Guitton, C. (2013). Cyber insecurity as a national threat: Overreaction from Germany, France and the UK? *European Security, 20*(1), 21–35.

Habermas, J. (1984). *The theory of communicative action*. London: Heinemann.

Habermas, J. (1996). *Between facts and norms: Contributions to a discourse theory of law and democracy*. Oxford: Polity Press.

Hansen, L., & Nissenbaum, H. (2009). Digital disaster, cyber security, and the Copenhagen School. *International Studies Quarterly, 53*(4), 1155–1175. doi:10.1111/j.1468-2478.2009. 00572.x.

Herschinger, E., & Renner, J. (Eds.). (2014). *Innovative Forschung: Vol. 1. Diskursforschung in den Internationalen Beziehungen*. Baden-Baden: Nomos Verl.-Ges.

Jasmontaite, L., & Pavel Burloiu, V. (2017). Lithuania and Romania to introduce cybersecurity laws. In W. J. Schünemann & M.-B. Baumann (Eds.), *Privacy, data protection and cybersecurity in Europe*. Cham: Springer.

Keller, R. (2008). *Wissenssoziologische Diskursanalyse. Grundlegung eines Forschungsprogramms* (2nd ed.). Wiesbaden: VS Verl. für Sozialwissenschaften.

Keller, R. (2013). *Doing discourse research: An introduction for social scientists*. London: Sage.

Nissenbaum, H. (2005). Where computer security meets national security. *Ethics and Information Technology, 7*(2), 61–73. doi:10.1007/s10676-005-4582-3.

Riedel, N. (2015, May 18). *Cyber security as a dimension of security policy*. Talk at Chatam House, London.

Singer, P. W., & Friedman, A. (2014). *Cybersecurity and cyberwar. What everyone needs to know*. Oxford: Oxford University Press.

Steiger, S. (2017). The unshaken role of GCHQ. In W. J. Schünemann & M.-B. Baumann (Eds.), *Privacy, data protection and cybersecurity in Europe*. Cham: Springer.

Steiger, S., Schünemann, W. J., & Dimmroth, K. (2017). Outrage without consequences? Post-Snowden discourses and governmental practice in Germany. *Media and Communication, 5*(1). doi:10.17645/mac.v5i1.814.

Steinmeier, F.-W. (2014a, June 12). *Digital society at stake—Europe and the future of the internet*. Talk at 7th European Dialogue on Internet Governance, New York.

Steinmeier, F.-W. (2014b, June 27). *Rede von Außenminister Frank-Walter Steinmeier beim Transatlantischen Cyber-Dialog, Berlin*.

Tiainen, M. (2017). Solving the surveillance problem. In W. J. Schünemann & M.-B. Baumann (Eds.), *Privacy, data protection and cybersecurity in Europe*. Cham: Springer.

Weiland, V. (2017). Analysing the French discourse about "surveillance and data protection" in the context of the NSA scandal. In W. J. Schünemann & M.-B. Baumann (Eds.), *Privacy, data protection and cybersecurity in Europe*. Cham: Springer.

Part III
Europeanisation: Centre and Periphery

Part III

Protecting or Processing?

Recasting EU Data Protection Norms

Ariadna Ripoll Servent

1 Introduction

The European Union (EU) is well-known for its high levels of data protection and concern about the effects of data sharing on individuals' privacy. The 1995 Data Protection Directive (95/46/EC) established clear norms that have guided the development of data protection laws at the national level. However, these principles have often been tested by advances in the field of law enforcement, where personal data has increasingly been processed for the purpose of fighting crime. Data protection has come much later into the security field and in a more diluted form than in the single market realm. As a result, two different logics have emerged over time: on the one hand, an 'economic' logic tended to concentrate on the negative effects that the single market might have on the protection of personal data and individual privacy. The process of easing cross-border flows of data in the private sector revealed important disparities between the levels of data protection at the national level and created pressure for further harmonisation. On the other hand, a 'security' logic dominated in the area of police and judicial cooperation in criminal matters: this logic underlined the importance of data processing, i.e. the use that internal security agencies can make of personal data in the interest of 'security'. In normative terms, the 'economic' logic largely reflects concerns about individual privacy, which led to the 'constitutionalisation' of data protection as a fundamental right in Article 16 of the Treaty on the Functioning of the European Union (TFEU) and Article 8 of the Charter of Fundamental Rights. In this sense, it often came into conflict with member states' normative understandings of the use of data in the public domain, especially in

A. Ripoll Servent (✉)
Universität Bamberg, Feldkirchenstr. 21, Bamberg 96045, Germany
e-mail: ariadna.ripoll@uni-bamberg.de

© Springer International Publishing AG 2017
W.J. Schünemann, M.-O. Baumann (eds.), *Privacy, Data Protection and Cybersecurity in Europe*, DOI 10.1007/978-3-319-53634-7_8

the field of law enforcement. There, the 'security' logic is more concerned with ensuring the safety of citizens than with protecting individual liberties.

Until 2009, these two logics had developed relatively independently of each other. While the 'economic' logic evolved within the framework of the single market (also known as the 'first pillar') in the shape of the Data Protection Directive (DPD) of 1995 (95/46/EC), the 'security' logic remained constrained by the intergovernmental rules prevailing in the field of police and criminal law matters (i.e. the EU's third pillar). The fact that laws had to be agreed upon unanimously by the member states and with almost no involvement by other EU institutions, such as the Commission or the European Parliament (EP), made it easier to keep the 'security' logic at the core of policy developments. However, with the enactment of the Treaty of Lisbon, the third pillar was abolished and police and criminal law matters were brought under the 'community method'. In practice, this meant that member states stopped being the sole decision-makers and had to share power with the European Parliament. It also underlined the necessity of bringing all data protection laws under one single umbrella.

The need to reform data protection laws revealed the profound normative differences that existed between private enterprise and the security field. The purpose of this chapter is, therefore, to determine how norms have been re-framed after the Treaty of Lisbon and to what extent a unified framework for EU data protection has been implemented. The first section of the chapter offers an overview of the main norms that prevailed under the first and third pillars before the enactment of the Treaty of Lisbon and how different actors promoted various (and sometimes conflicting) understandings of personal data. The second section reviews the efforts of core policymakers to find common understandings of data protection during the reform process. It concentrates first on negotiations for a new General Regulation on Data Protection (hereafter the 'Regulation') and examines later the more specific Data Protection Directive for law enforcement (hereafter the 'Directive') in order to assess to what extent the tensions between data protection and data processing have been solved in the course of negotiations. The empirical data was gathered from official documents, public debates and interviews with members of the European Parliament, Commission, Council and permanent representations. The semi-structured interviews were done in Brussels in April 2014, February 2015 and May 2016.

2   Data Protection and Data Processing Before the Treaty of Lisbon

The emergence of data protection as a policy issue is closely linked to developments at the EU level. When the DPD was introduced in 1995, data protection was absent in most member states and the EU was responsible for building up a new legislative and normative framework. In these decisive moments of norm definition, the purpose of data protection was linked to the single market project and aimed at improving the free flow of personal data across EU member states. This came as a result of functional developments: the single market and Schengen revealed gaps in the legislation and forced the Commission to propose a common EU solution (De Hert et al. 2008; Newman 2008; Pearce and Platten 1998). The DPD became a clear translation of the Commission's efforts to create common standards and, most importantly, a common definition of data protection (Commission official, interview April 2014). Although this common normative frame was gradually accepted by national actors and incorporated into domestic legislation, its reach remained nevertheless limited to data protection in the economic field.

When it comes to the field of security, it was not until 2005 that the Commission drafted an instrument dealing with data protection in the field of law enforcement. When this happened, the norms that guided the legislative process were clearly different from those of the DPD. This was due mostly to the changing political environment, particularly after the attacks of 11 September 2001, which led member states to become more active in the area of police and criminal law cooperation. There, the normative context coming from the US and various member states stressed the use of data to fight terrorism and other types of organised crime. The US' taste for connecting personal data through databases and using them for purposes other than those envisaged at their outset created numerous conflicts with EU legislation. Cases such as the Passenger Name Records saga, Safe Harbour or SWIFT highlighted the difficulties in keeping the private and public spheres separate and stressed the tension between data protection and data processing (Argomaniz 2009; Long and Quek 2002; Ripoll Servent and MacKenzie 2011). When negotiating with the US, the main difficulties for the EU revolved around the low level of protection offered by US legislation, especially to non-US citizens, and the reluctance of US authorities to change their domestic legal standards.

At the same time, EU member states were not setting a much better example. Despite the growing need to regulate the use of personal data for law enforcement purposes, member states remained overwhelmingly cautious and unwilling to regulate the use of personal data by national law enforcement authorities (De Hert et al. 2008). During the 2000s, there was rapid development of security tools based on the pooling and sharing of personal data. The Data Retention Directive (2006/24/EC), the Schengen Information System (reformed in 2006/7) or the Prüm Convention (2005) are some of the most notorious examples. More importantly, the 'security' logic was expanded to instruments that had been initiated in the economic realm to protect consumers from abuses in the private sector. In 2002, for instance, a revision of the Data Protection in the Telecommunications Sector Directive (e-Privacy Directive 2002/58/EC) was introduced in the first pillar as part of the single market strategy. The overall objective of this directive was to regulate the storage of personal data by private companies and to avoid abuses of consumers' data. However, member states managed to introduce a new clause in Article 15.1, which allowed them to broaden the types of data stored and to use them for security purposes.

The conflict between the 'economic' and 'security' understandings of personal data peaked during negotiations on the Data Retention Directive (2006/24/EC), which allowed the storage of personal telecommunications data (obtained from the private sector) for the investigation and prosecution of serious crimes. The directive was a clear example of the tensions between data protection and data processing, as well as between the use of data in the private (e.g. by companies) and public sector. This tension was visible in the long conflict surrounding its legal basis: both a third-pillar text (i.e. in the framework of law enforcement cooperation) and a proposal for a first-pillar directive (as part of the single market for telecommunications) were negotiated in parallel until almost the last moment. In the end, the Council accepted a first-pillar text that was very close to its own security interests and concerns. The largest groups in the European Parliament accepted the deal in the hope that it would help them convince the Council of the necessity of regulating data processing in the field of police and judicial cooperation in criminal matters (Ripoll Servent 2013). The final deal did not actually solve the tension that arose from using an economic instrument for data processing purposes. On the contrary, this normative impasse was left to the European Court of Justice, which did not contest the principle of retaining data for law enforcement purposes per se, but did contest the lack of proportionality inherent in the text and declared it invalid (European Court of Justice 2014b).

In the meantime, the European Parliament continued to push for better regulation of data protection in law enforcement. Member states reluctantly reached an agreement in 2008 on a Framework Decision for data protection in the area of police and judicial cooperation in criminal matters (2008/977/JHA).[1] As mentioned above, the Council had always been reticent to regulate the use of data in this field, and it was only due to the insistence of the EP that the instrument saw light. In fact, the EP rejected several proposals made by the Council because they did not go far enough in the protection of personal data. The EP tried to change the last version of the decision by introducing higher standards of data protection and linking the proposal to existing data protection instruments such as the DPD. Although the Council dismissed most of these modifications, the efforts of the EP demonstrate its willingness to create an instrument that would constrain the use of personal data for processing purposes (De Hert and Papakonstantinou 2009; EDRI 2009). In the end, member states agreed only on the most basic of provisions, which meant that the Framework Decision only affected cross-border data and excluded data shared among different national authorities of one single member state. On this occasion, the EP had only the right to produce a non-binding opinion and could not introduce any substantive amendments to the text.

---

[1] A Framework Decision is the term given to the old legal instruments of the third pillar. They are similar to a Directive but have different legal effects (especially when it comes to scrutiny by the Court of Justice) and were decided under unanimity of member states, after a (non-binding) opinion of the European Parliament.

The Treaty of Lisbon instituted essential changes to the data protection architecture. Data protection became a fundamental right in Article 16 TFEU and Article 8 of the Charter of Fundamental Rights, which meant that it legally prevailed over other objectives such as the single market. It also meant that, in case of conflict, the Court of Justice would have to take the Treaty and the Charter of Fundamental Rights into account. In addition, the Treaty caused the end of the pillar structure; the former third pillar was mostly *communitarised*, which meant that police and judicial cooperation in criminal matters would now be decided on under co-decision and qualified majority voting in the Council. In view of these changes, it is important to understand how the two logics of data protection have been reconciled in the context of a major reform of EU data protection legislation.

3 Data Protection Norms After the Treaty of Lisbon

The reform of the two main data protection instruments was initiated as a response to the general claim that the 1995 DPD was largely outdated and did not fit the technological and social developments of the last decade. Businesses wanted a clearer and harmonised approach to data protection that would also provide more certainty for both enterprises and consumers. With this objective in mind, the Commission presented a legislative package at the end of 2012 with the aim of having it negotiated and agreed upon before the end of the parliamentary term in 2014 (EU official, interview April 2014). It decided to transform the 1995 DPD into a regulation that would cover the use of data both in the private and the public sector (European Commission 2012b) and to upgrade the Framework Decision into a directive that would apply not only to cross-border exchanges of data but also to data processing inside each member state (European Commission 2012a). Therefore, the Commission planned to erase the different definitions and uses of data protection in the private and public sector to the greatest possible extent, and to further a common understanding of personal data across the economic and security realms. The aim was to achieve more harmonisation and free flows of data, which should improve trust among member states (Commission official, interview April 2014).

The Regulation contained various controversial points, mostly regarding the scope and categories of data as well as the degree of harmonisation. The Directive, on the other hand, re-established certain elements that had already been proposed in the 2005 proposal for a Framework Decision and later been dismissed by member states. There, the main issues referred to the administrative burden and the practical application of several measures proposed by the Commission (Axel Voss, EPP MEP; diplomatic source A, interviews April 2014). The proposals were transmitted to the EP and the Council, which initiated negotiations inside each institution with the objective of reaching a unified institutional position. It quickly became clear that member states had crucial concerns about the reform package and that negotiations would not proceed as quickly as it had been expected. Within the EP, negotiations also took longer than usual and were riddled with difficulties. With the Commission putting pressure on the different political groups and the 2014 elections approaching (Speiser, EPP political advisor; EP staff A, interviews April 2014), the EP managed to reach a common position on both the Regulation and the Directive in November 2013 (European Parliament 2013a, b)—eventually voted on in plenary on 12 March 2014. The Regulation received the overwhelming support of all political groups in the Chamber, with 621 votes for, 10 against and 22 abstentions. In turn, the Directive was supported by a left/liberal coalition with 371 votes for, 276 against and 30 abstentions. The centre and right-wing groups opposed the EP position as stated in the report but supported the mandate to continue negotiations with the Council in the LIBE Committee.[2] By early 2014, it became clear that no agreement could be reached before the elections and, thus, the texts were put on hold until June 2015, when trialogues[3] started for the Regulation. The Council only reached a Common Position on the Directive at the beginning of October 2015 and trialogues were rapidly conducted until the end of 2015. A political agreement was reached for both the Regulation and the Directive on 15 December 2015; they were finally voted on in Council on 8 April and in Parliament on 14 April 2016.

After these long and difficult negotiations, is there still tension between the 'economic' and the 'security' logic in data protection? How close has the EU come to formulating common EU norms on data protection? The next sections examine the main normative conflicts in the Regulation and the Directive and the extent to which these have been resolved in the final agreement.

4   Negotiations on the General Data Protection Regulation

The reform of the DPD has been one of the major legislative efforts of the EU in the last few years. The Regulation became a very complex text and received high levels of attention from policy-makers and beyond. Indeed, the 3999 amendments proposed by the EP to the Commission's text reflect the widespread pressure coming from interest groups and domestic constituencies (Euractiv 2016). The Regulation (2016/679) offers common standards for data protection and is directly applicable to the national level. It offers the main framework of reference when it comes to protecting the use of personal data both in the private sector and by public authorities. It settles highly disputed issues, such as the definition of 'personal data'; how to deal with 'anonymised' or 'pseudonymised' data (as well as the connected

---

[2]The LIBE Committee voted in favour of a negotiating mandate for the directive with 47 votes in favour, 4 against and 1 abstention (European Parliament 2014a: 8).

[3]Trialogues (or trilogues) are informal negotiations held between a team of negotiators from the Council and the European Parliament (and the participation of the Commission) with the aim of reaching an agreement that can receive the support of member states and the EP's plenary (for further information, see Roederer-Rynning and Greenwood 2015).

issue of profiling); the 'right to be forgotten' (now called 'right to erasure'); the portability of personal data; sanctions for companies as well as the transfer of data to third-countries (for more information, see Council of the European Union 2015; European Parliament 2014a). One of the main innovations is the general principle of data protection 'by design and by default' (Article 25), which means that the protection of personal data has to be integrated into the development of any new service or business and that the highest protection possible is offered automatically to citizens when they need to provide personal data, without any need for them to actively seek higher privacy settings.

These specific provisions, however, hide underlying discussions on the main purpose and scope of the Regulation. On the one hand, there were profound normative cleavages concerning the definition and pre-eminence of data protection over other interests. Discussions in the European Parliament started from a 'liberty' perspective that was anchored in debates around the right balance between 'liberty' and 'security'. This was not unexpected, since debates took place in the Civil Liberties and Justice and Home Affairs Committee (LIBE), which had witnessed various conflicts around data protection in the past (Ripoll Servent 2015). In addition, the EP's rapporteur[4] (Jan Philipp Albrecht, Germany) was a member of the Green group and well-known for his strong views on privacy and data protection. Therefore, most actors involved in negotiations suspected that he might take a 'radical' view on data protection reform, which might have hindered consensus across political groups and with the Council (Commission official; EU official, interviews April 2014). Indeed, left-wing groups adopted an understanding of data protection based on the 'liberty vs. security' cleavage that had already characterised past interinstitutional conflicts: they stressed the fact that European courts would now have to evaluate data processing in the light of the Charter of fundamental rights and the TFEU principles to anchor data protection into a fundamental rights framework (S&D political advisor, interview April 2014).

These high standards were considered too 'idealistic' by centrist and right-wing parties (Speiser, EPP political advisor; Axel Voss, EPP MEP, interviews April 2014), which shifted the debate towards a different understanding of 'liberty'. Their understanding of the problem did not come from a 'security' rationale but rather from an 'economic' rationale: liberals and conservatives were worried that the high standards demanded by the greens and social-democrats would end up as a heavy burden on European businesses (Speiser, EPP political advisor; MEP assistant, EP staff A, interviews April 2014). By doing so, they brought the conflict back to the 'economic' logic and started speaking of a conflict between 'consumers' and 'companies' (MEP assistant, interview, April 2014). These different understandings triggered long negotiations, since they emphasised the role of business interests and

---

[4]Rapporteurs are the MEPs responsible for writing the EP report, which contains the amendments proposed to the Commission's proposal. They also head the EP's negotiating team when it comes to finding an agreement with the Council. Shadow rapporteurs are MEPs from other political groups that follow and participate in negotiations.

raised the need for more expertise on the potential costs for European companies. The LIBE committee spent almost 10 months discussing the content of the Regulation, during which negotiators had to find a difficult balance between gathering expertise while filtering huge amounts of information provided by interest groups (Speiser, EPP political advisor; EP staff A, interviews April 2014). In the end, negotiations turned into a collective effort to find a normative frame that could be accepted by a majority of political groups. Therefore, the efforts of the rapporteur and shadow rapporteurs focused on finding a 'balance' between 'idealists' and 'realists'—i.e. those who put more emphasis on high data protection standards vs. those who wished to simplify the rules and ensure that the regulation would not slow down the EU's economic activity (Speiser, EPP political advisor, interview April 2014). The Justice Commissioner (Viviane Reding at the time) underlined the main rationales behind the EP first-reading position, namely

> It will give individuals control over their own data and restore lost trust. It equips regulators with strong enforcement powers and it allows companies to exploit the full potential of the digital economy (European Parliament 2014b).

The 'companies' frame was even more present in the Council, where member states were concerned about how EP amendments (e.g. 'informed consent', 'privacy by design') might increase the red tape faced by companies (Speiser, EPP political advisor, interview February 2015). Around March 2015, it was clear that most member states were trying to dilute central aspects of the Regulation (such as the 'purpose limitation' and 'data minimisation' principles) to the point that 40% of the changes went below the standards of the 1995 DPD; even member states that were considered to have concerns about high data protection standards (notably Germany) showed a close relationship with lobbyists and proposed mostly business-friendly amendments, such as the possibility to use data without explicit consent for marketing or to assess someone's credit worthiness (Euobserver 2015).

However, the elements that created the most controversy and slowed down negotiations primarily concerned the scope of the Regulation as well as the level of harmonisation. Two elements of the Regulation served to channel this conflict: concerns about its impact on member states' public administrations and the extent of the Commission's power in settling potential infringements. The first element came as a direct consequence of the DPD's success in shaping member states' domestic norms in the field of data protection: when the 95/46/EC Directive had been approved, member states generally lacked national legislation on personal data; in 2012, there were better developed data protection systems at the national level but also more intrinsic differences in the understanding of personal data among them (EU official, interview April 2014). Those that had more developed data protection systems (mostly Northern European countries) were reluctant to harmonise further and accept a Regulation that could be directly applicable not just to the private sector but also to national public authorities (diplomatic source A, interview April 2014; EU official, interview February 2015). Member states were, therefore, generally unhappy with the choice of legal instrument, considering that a regulation would be too detailed and could not be directly implemented in many practical situations, particularly in regard to the public sector (Euobserver 2013, 2014 EP staff A; MEP assistant; Speiser, EPP political advisor; EU official, interviews April 2014). While no-one doubted the benefits that the Regulation could bring to the private sector, member states started pointing out that the same instruments could not be used for the public use of data, especially with issues such as 'data portability', consent and the 'right to be forgotten' (EU official; diplomatic source A, interviews April 2014).

A change in the actors dealing with negotiations in the Council also explains how this conflict became more dominant among member states. While, at the beginning, foreign ministers had dealt with the file in the isolated framework of the General Affairs Council, from 2014, national ministries and data protection authorities started to pay more attention to the different drafts coming from the Commission and the EP (S&D political advisor, interview April 2014). As a result, many national governments raised reservations and it was decided to stop negotiations. As an EU diplomat put it, 'the code word is always "this is too important" to take hasty decisions' (in Euobserver 2013). This decision was supported primarily by Germany, which found that a regulation would not fit with the multiplicity of data protection provisions as befits its federal system and that the text should be changed into a directive (Euractiv 2015a Speiser, EPP political advisor; Axel Voss, EPP MEP; diplomatic source A, interviews April 2014; EU official, interview February 2015). Indeed, although this issue had gone mostly unnoticed in the EP, some German delegations from different political groups had already warned about the potential implications for their country (EP staff A, S&D political advisor, interviews April 2014). It was only in autumn 2014, when the German government decided that it was better to have an imperfect agreement than no agreement at all that negotiations could start again and a deadline for the end of 2015 was fixed (Der Tagesspiegel 2014).

However, the reluctance of member states came not just as a reaction to the dispositions on public services, but also to the perception that the Commission had chosen a regulation as the legal instrument so that it could increase its control over the implementation and monitoring process (EU official, interview April 2014). This conflict became apparent in the debate surrounding the inclusion of a 'one-stop-shop' principle. This idea had been widely supported by tech companies, which preferred to deal with only one national Data Protection Authority (DPA), instead of 28 different ones (Fontanella-Khan 2013). The proposal foresaw a more coordinated role of national DPAs and the creation of a 'European Data Protection Board' (EDPB). In the original text, DPAs would have to cooperate with the Commission through a 'consistency mechanism',[5] which was seen as a step too far in the Commission's attempts to harmonise data protection. The EP substituted the supervisory role of the Commission by placing the EDPB as core arbiter. National parliaments also raised concerns regarding the subsidiarity effects of such a measure,

---

[5]Eventually included in a modified version in Articles 63–67.

although their claims were largely influenced by national DPAs, which were afraid of losing their power (EU official, interview April 2014).

Therefore, the one-stop-shop principle reflected the reaction of member states towards harmonisation: for some, such as Germany, Hungary, Denmark and the Czech Republic, it meant risking high levels of data protection (diplomatic source A, interview April 2014) and revealed the lack of trust on the decisions taken by other DPAs (Euractiv 2013). For the UK, Denmark, Hungary, and Slovenia, it also reflected the intrusive nature of the Commission and was an example of the inadequacy of a regulation as a general framework for data protection (Commission official, interview April 2014). After going back and forth, the Council's general approach opted for appointing a 'lead authority' in charge of coordinating with other DPAs. However, this 'lead authority' would be able to opt out of a case and leave it to other authorities. In the end, the Regulation (see Articles 60–62) leaves the EDPB in a weaker position (only in charge of 'serious' cases) and devises a complex system that might not prevent the need to deal with multiple DPAs (European Voice 2015; Global Data Hub 2015).

The Regulation, therefore, has managed to update and harmonise the understanding of 'data protection' to a large extent for both the private and public sector. This is an important step, since it means that the Regulation will have an impact not only on how private companies but also public administrations deal with personal data. In this respect, the Regulation was successful in creating a single normative framework that enhances the rights of individuals when it comes to protecting their personal data. However, despite a clear effort to integrate the law enforcement field into the same normative framework, negotiations failed to produce a common understanding of data protection for the internal market and the security field.

5   The Directive for Law Enforcement

In comparison to the long and intense negotiations on the Regulation, the Directive (2016/680) has received much less attention, both within the institutions and in public discussions. This was surprising, especially when it came to the European Parliament, which had fought hard and long for the 2008 Framework Decision (Commission official, interview April 2014). The lack of salience might have been due to a variety of reasons. Firstly, there was a generalised agreement that the Directive touched on very sensitive data, but that, after all, it was 'only' a directive subordinated to the Regulation (EP staff B, interview April 2014). Secondly, the first rapporteur (Droutsas, Greek social-democrat) was seen as less involved and more unreliable than Albrecht (EP staff A; EU official, interviews April 2014). Thirdly, negotiations were led mostly by the social-democrats and the liberals; the latter were represented by Sophie in 't Veld (Netherlands), who held a more left-wing and pro-data protection position than most MEPs in her group (EP staff A; Axel Voss, EPP MEP, interviews April 2014). Furthermore, the conservatives were mostly absent from negotiations and only made their interests clear when a broad agreement had been reached (S&D political advisor; EP staff A and B, interviews April 2014). Therefore, there were fewer disagreements among the group of negotiators, who all agreed on the idea of treating the Directive as part of a 'package'. In practice, the 'package' logic emphasised harmonisation and the predominance of the Regulation ('lex generalis') over the Directive, which should then only specify substantive differences related to law enforcement ('lex specialis').

The first rapporteur underlined the importance of the 'package' approach by affirming that

> Parliament has been calling for years for a comprehensive single instrument on data protection that would cover both the private and the public sectors, including the police and judicial cooperation in criminal matters. This is why this Parliament has always, right from the beginning, regarded the proposed regulation and directive as a package: what we call the 'package approach', and all our legislative work on the data protection reform has been conducted on precisely this premise (Droutsas in European Parliament 2014c).

This political frame translated into a very pragmatic practice: the two rapporteurs sat together and proceeded to copy and paste the dispositions that had already been agreed upon in the Regulation into the text of the Directive (EP staff A and B; MEP assistant, interviews April 2014). As a result, the negotiating mandate underlined that 'a number of concepts envisaged in the regulation, such as profiling, explicit consent, using clear, simple language and appointing a data protection officer, should also apply to the directive' (European Parliament 2014a: 6). Thus, the EP's approach went further than the Commission, which had not included elements such as 'explicit consent' in the directive.

The success of the 'package approach' was not straightforward. There were many criticisms coming from inside both the EP and the Council. The conservative groups in the EP raised concerns regarding the applicability of certain changes (Speiser, EPP political advisor, interview April 2014), such as the introduction of explicit consent in recital one or the possibility for data subjects to redress or correct their information. They considered that the nature of the Regulation and the Directive were so different that a copy-paste approach could not work (Speiser, EPP political advisor, interview April 2014). Axel Voss, shadow rapporteur for the EPP group, expressed this view in the plenary debate preceding the first-reading vote:

> A social network needs other rules as a police authority—for the former we need a Regulation, for the latter a Directive—in my opinion, a Directive that takes the form of the 2008 Framework Decision. If we could upgrade it into a directive, it would be in fact the best solution (Voss in European Parliament 2014c).

Their position resonated with the majority of member states, which were reluctant to transform the 2008 Framework Decision into a Directive. The attempt to find common standards became increasingly contested, particularly by Interior Ministers (Commission official, interview April 2014). In some cases, it was considered that the system proposed by the Commission would be too unwieldy and would hinder rather than foster cooperation in this domain (Hohlmeier, EPP MEP, interview February 2015; diplomatic source B, interview May 2016). Other member states such as Germany, Austria and Slovenia were afraid that the Directive would lower data protection standards and create discrepancies during the implementation process (Giovanni Buttarelli, EDPS, interview May 2016). They were thus reluctant to share personal data with other member states perceived as too lax with the protection of personal data. As a result, the Council remained firmly opposed to the need for more EU legislation in such a sensitive area, especially when the 2008 Framework Decision had only just been implemented (2008/977/JHA, Article 27) and member states had not yet had any practical experience in dealing with data protection in the law enforcement field (Speiser, EPP political advisor; EU official, interviews April 2014; diplomatic source B, Council officials, interviews May 2016). Since the Directive was not seen as an essential instrument, member states' motto was to 'do as little as possible' (diplomatic source B, interview May 2016).

Interestingly, however, the preference for stability and inaction started to erode due to events unfolding outside the context of negotiations. On the one hand, the attacks in Paris in January and November 2015 put member states under pressure to re-start discussions on the Directive, which had hardly appeared on the Council's agenda since 2012 (Bowman 2015, Council officials, interview May 2016). For instance, on 'Data Protection Day', Commission Vice-President Andrus Ansip and Commissioner Věra Jourová issued a Joint Statement that underlined

> EU Data Protection reform also includes new rules for police and criminal justice author-
> ities when they exchange data across the EU. This is very timely, not least in light of the
> recent terrorist attacks in Paris. There is need to continue and to intensify our law
> enforcement cooperation. Robust data protection rules will foster more effective coopera-
> tion based on mutual trust (European Commission 2015).

On the other hand, the Snowden revelations and several European Court of Justice (ECJ) rulings related to data processing also raised the urgency to regulate the use of data processing by law enforcement. In April 2014, the ECJ declared the Data Retention Directive invalid due to its lack of proportionality (European Court of Justice 2014a). More recently, the Schrems decision questioned the generalised access of public authorities to electronic communications and stressed the need to include strict conditions for the transfer of data to third countries (European Court of Justice 2015).

Therefore, albeit reluctantly, member states started to look for a new solution that would still fit their shared norms on data processing. The solution came through a two fold strategy. First, the EP accepted a watered down version of the proposal while insisting on the 'package approach', which prevented the Council from dropping the Directive altogether. By linking the two files and sticking to the deadline of 2015, the EP put pressure on the Latvian and (particularly) Luxem-bourgish presidencies. In a way, the EP engaged in a quid pro quo strategy. They agreed to step up efforts on the Regulation only if member states ensured that the Directive would also be discussed and agreed upon: no Regulation without Direc-tive. The 'package approach', therefore, ensured that by mid-2015 negotiations started in earnest in the Council, where there were two or three meetings of expert groups organised every week—a high rate in comparison to normal Council negotiations (diplomatic source B, interview May 2016). This approach also ensured that the core principles achieved in the Regulation—most notably the idea of data protection by design and by default—were also present in the Directive. Even representatives of member states came to accept that it might be a good idea to mimic the Regulation as much as possible, since the rights of the individual were the same in both (diplomatic source B, interview May 2016).

However, the final agreement was also made possible because the Council managed to emphasise the 'security' aspects of the Directive and introduced as much flexibility as possible for processing personal data in the law enforcement field (Sargentini, Green MEP, interview February 2015). The main aim of the member states was to leave law enforcement authorities 'unencumbered' in the fight against serious crime. This message resonated well with conservative groups in the EP. For instance, immediately after the Paris attacks on 13 November 2015, Axel Voss (shadow rapporteur for the EPP group) called for the suspension of trialogues, justifying this on the following grounds:

> My political group has been highly sceptical about the Data Protection Directive proposal from the very beginning ... the text stipulates major bureaucratic burdens to law enforcement and security entities and would basically transform them into data protection officers when processing personal data for the purpose of prevention, investigation, detection or prosecution of criminal offences and terrorist activities ... The Paris terrorist attacks have shown that the security of our citizens has to prevail over bureaucracy! (European People's Party 2015).

As a result, the key issue of individual consent was deleted from the Directive and the scope was extended to cover 'threats to public security' (the term is, however, not defined in Article 1), while excluding activities that fall outside EU law (which means that intelligence services are out of the Directive's reach, see Article 2). It also provides such a broad definition of 'competent authorities' (Article 3.7) that it could potentially include private parties such as airlines or financial institutions. There are also other erosions when it comes to the 'purpose limitation' principle, the rights of data subjects, the role of DPAs and the transfer of data to third countries (see also the report by the European Data Protection Supervisor 2015).

6 Conclusion

The reform of the Data Protection Package has proved one of the most challenging files of this legislature. It is interesting to see that, despite the changes in the inter-institutional balance of power, the normative frames prevailing inside each institution have not changed substantially. The EP is generally more prone to emphasise data protection as a fundamental right, while the Council is still more concerned about data processing and its impact on security. However, even these findings need to be nuanced. First, the EP's defence of data protection has been influenced by the presence of social-democrats and Greens as its main negotiators. If these positions had been held by conservative groups, we might have seen a more diluted data protection reform—closer to member states' concerns. We have seen how the centre-right groups have been more insistent on the potential big data might offer and have joined the Council in calling for a 'risk-based approach' to data protection (Euractiv 2015b). Their support for the 'security' logic has been most evident in the Directive, where they have contributed to watering down and deleting some provisions that might have had a direct impact on the ability of law enforcement to process data and use profiling tools (cf. The Parliament Magazine 2015).

Second, one can observe that the main divide inside and across EU institutions has been over the shape and necessity of new legislation, even more than over the content of specific provisions. When it comes to the Regulation, the Council stressed the need for more flexible solutions, even though this runs against the rationale of using a regulation to provide common standards. As for the Directive, member states questioned the necessity of a new legislative instrument, which shows how reluctant they were to introduce further coordination in the field of law enforcement and the remaining gaps in trust among national authorities. It is, however, interesting to see that episodes stemming from the two sides of the 'liberty vs. security' logic—namely the Snowden revelations on the one side and the terror attacks in Paris on the other—created enough pressure to break their inaction and facilitated the conclusion of negotiations over a short span of time.

The final outcome is a clear compromise made possible by the 'package approach' but also by the manifold exceptions aimed at leaving national authorities a large amount of room to manoeuvre. This means that, though now having a more unified framework for data protection, the tension between the principles of privacy and security has not been resolved and could emerge again in future negotiations that touch upon data processing and the use of personal data, like the reform of the 2002 e-Privacy Directive. As Jan Albrecht stated at the end of the negotiations:

> The next big step is that we need to get it right with regard to the core of privacy and civil liberties in the digital society, which means we need to evaluate surveillance measures and adjust them to what we see as a liberal democracy (in Euractiv 2016).

References

Argomaniz, J. (2009). When the EU is the 'Norm-taker': The passenger name records agreement and the EU's internalization of US border security norms. *Journal of European Integration, 31*(1), 119–136.

Bowman, J. (2015, February 6). Paris attacks bring 'Police' directive negotiations back into spotlight. *The privacy advisor*. Retrieved November 18, 2015, from https://iapp.org/news/a/paris-attacks-bring-police-directive-negotiations-back-into-spotlight/

Council of the European Union. (2015). Council document of 11 June 2015, note from the presidency, 9565/15.

De Hert, P., & Papakonstantinou, V. (2009). The data protection framework decision of 27 November 2008 regarding police and judicial cooperation in criminal matters – A modest achievement however not the improvement some have hoped for. *Computer Law & Security Review, 25*(5), 403–414.

De Hert, P., Papakonstantinou, V., & Riehle, C. (2008). Data protection in the third pillar: Cautious pessimism. In M. Maik (Ed.), *Crime, rights and the EU: The future of police and judicial cooperation* (pp. 121–194). London: Justice.

Der Tagesspiegel. (2014, October 8). *Deutschland erwägt, Google Löschkriterien vorzugeben.* Retrieved November 17, 2015, from http://www.tagesspiegel.de/themen/agenda/europaeische-datenschutzverordnung-deutschland-erwaegt-google-loeschkriterien-vorzugeben/10809162.html

EDRI. (2009, February 11). Data protection framework decision adopted. *EDRI-gram, 7*(3). http://www.edri.org/edri-gram/number7.3/data-protection-framework-decision

Euobserver. (2013, December 6). *EU data protection bill 'Moves Backwards'.* Retrieved April 6, 2014, from http://euobserver.com/justice/122384

Euobserver. (2014, January 24). *EU data bill delayed until after may elections.* Retrieved April 6, 2014, from http://euobserver.com/justice/122853

Euobserver. (2015, March 11). *German-led moves to weaken EU data bill a 'Scandal'.* Retrieved November 17, 2015, from https://euobserver.com/justice/127961

Euractiv. (2013, December 9). *Data protection reform in Peril as Germany stymies deal.* Retrieved April 6, 2014, from http://www.euractiv.com/infosociety/data-protection-reform-peril-ger-news-532189

Euractiv. (2015a, January 8). *EU lawmaker warns of data protection rules delay till 2016.* Retrieved November 12, 2015, from http://www.euractiv.com/sections/infosociety/eu-law maker-warns-data-protection-rules-delay-till-2016-311100

Euractiv. (2015b, June 25). *We need to make big data into an opportunity for Europe.* Retrieved November 18, 2015, from http://www.euractiv.com/sections/infosociety/we-need-make-big-data-opportunity-europe-315750

Euractiv. (2016, April 14). *Parliament approves privacy rules after record number of amendments.* Retrieved May 24, 2016, from http://www.euractiv.com/section/digital/news/parlia ment-approves-privacy-rules-after-record-number-of-amendments/

European Commission. (2012a, January 25). Proposal for a directive of the European parliament and of the council on the protection of individuals with regard to the processing of personal data by competent authorities for the purposes of prevention, investigation, detection or prosecution of criminal offences or the execution of criminal penalties, and the free movement of such data, COM/2012/010 final.

European Commission. (2012b, December 25). Proposal for a regulation of the European parliament and of the council on the protection of individuals with regard to the processing of personal data and on the free movement of such data (General Data Protection Regulation), COM/2012/011 final.

European Commission. (2015, January 28). Press release. *Data protection day 2015: Concluding the EU data protection reform essential for the digital single market.* Retrieved November 18, 2015, from http://europa.eu/rapid/press-release_MEMO-15-3802_en.htm

European Court of Justice. (2014a, April 8). Judgment in joined Cases C-293/12 and C-594/12 digital rights Ireland and seitlinger and others.

European Court of Justice. (2014b, April 8). The court of justice declares the data retention directive to be invalid, Press Release No 54/14.

European Court of Justice. (2015, October 6). Maximillian Schrems v data protection commissioner, Case C-362/14.

European Data Protection Supervisor. (2015). *A further step towards comprehensive EU data protection: EDPS recommendations on the directive for data protection in the police and justice sectors* (No. Opinion 6/2015). Retrieved November 18, 2015, from https://secure.edps. europa.eu/EDPSWEB/webdav/site/mySite/shared/Documents/Consultation/Opinions/2015/ 15-10-28_Directive_Recommendations_EN.pdf

European Parliament. (2013a, November 22). Report of 22 November 2013 on the proposal for a regulation of the European parliament and of the council on the protection of individuals with regard to the processing of personal data and on the free movement of such data (General Data Protection Regulation), A7-0402/2013.

European Parliament. (2013b, November 22). Report of 22 November 2013 on the proposal for a directive of the European parliament and of the council on the protection of individuals with regard to the processing of personal data by competent authorities for the purposes of prevention, investigation, detection or prosecution of criminal offences or the execution of criminal penalties, and the free movement of such data, A7-0403/2013.

European Parliament. (2014a, March 4). Q&A on EU data protection reform. *European Parliament*. Retrieved April 6, 2014, from http://www.europarl.europa.eu/news/en/news-room/content/20130502BKG07917/pdf

European Parliament. (2014b, March 11). *Data protection package and NSA surveillance: 'Europe needs a digital Bill of Rights'*. Retrieved April 6, 2014, from http://www.europarl.europa.eu/news/en/news-room/content/20140311IPR38601/pdf

European Parliament. (2014c, March 11). Debates - Tuesday, 11 March 2014 - Protection of individuals with regard to the processing of personal data - Processing of personal data for the purposes of crime prevention, CRE 11/03/2014-13. Retrieved April 6, 2014, from http://www.europarl.europa.eu/sides/getDoc.do?type=CRE&reference=20140311&secondRef=ITEM-013&language=EN&ring=A7-2013-0403

European People's Party. (2015, November 16). *Data protection directive trialogue should be suspended*. Retrieved November 18, 2015, from http://www.eppgroup.eu/press-release/Data-Protection-Directive-trialogue-should-be-suspended

European Voice. (2015, March 13). *Ministers sign up for controversial one-stop-shop for data protection*. Retrieved November 17, 2015, from http://www.politico.eu/article/ministers-sign-up-for-one-stop-shop-for-data-protection/

Fontanella-Khan, J. (2013, December 6). EU data protection rules hit by surprise legal objection. *Financial Times*. Retrieved April 6, 2014, from http://www.ft.com/cms/s/0/6930c9a6-5e8a-11e3-8621-00144feabdc0.html

Global Data Hub. (2015, October). *The 'one stop shop'*. Retrieved November 17, 2015, from http://united-kingdom.taylorwessing.com/globaldatahub/article-one-stop-shop.html

Long, W. J., & Quek, M. P. (2002). Personal data privacy protection in an age of globalization: The US-EU safe harbor compromise. *Journal of European Public Policy, 9*(3), 325–344.

Newman, A. L. (2008). Building transnational civil liberties: Transgovernmental entrepreneurs and the European data privacy directive. *International Organization, 62*(1), 103–130.

Pearce, G., & Platten, N. (1998). Achieving personal data protection in the European Union. *Journal of Common Market Studies, 36*(4), 529–547.

Ripoll Servent, A. (2013). Holding the European Parliament responsible: Policy shift in the data retention directive from consultation to codecision. *Journal of European Public Policy, 20*(7), 972–987.

Ripoll Servent, A. (2015). *Institutional and policy change in the European Parliament: Deciding on freedom, security and justice*. Houndmills: Palgrave MacMillan.

Ripoll Servent, A., & MacKenzie, A. (2011). Is the EP still a data protection champion? The case of SWIFT. *Perspectives on European Politics and Society, 12*(4), 390–406.

Roederer-Rynning, C., & Greenwood, J. (2015). The culture of trilogues. *Journal of European Public Policy, 22*(8), 1148–1165.

The Parliament Magazine. (2015, July 3). *EU Parliament's largest political groups split over fundamental rights*. Retrieved May 25, 2016, from https://www.theparliamentmagazine.eu/articles/news/eu-parliaments-largest-political-groups-split-over-fundamental-rights

Lithuania and Romania to Introduce Cybersecurity Laws

Attaining Information Security at the Cost of Individuals' Rights

Lina Jasmontaite and Valentina Pavel Burloiu

1 Introduction

The perception of cybersecurity has changed over time, and it currently comprises technical, legal and policy measures. The concept has expanded greatly since its initial scope, which focused on information technologies and referred to the security requirements of an information system, namely availability, integrity and confidentiality. According to the most exhaustive definition introduced by the International Telecommunication Union (ITU), cybersecurity consists of "the collection of tools, policies, security concepts, security safeguards, guidelines, risk management approaches, actions, training, best practices, assurance and technologies that can be used to protect the cyber environment and organisation and user's assets" (ITU, 04/08). As per ITU, users' assets may entail technology, personnel, telecommunication systems and transmission of data (ITU, 04/08). The chapter builds on this definition.

In order to address regulatory and legal issues arising in the context of cybersecurity regulation, this chapter employs two different approaches to examine Lithuanian and Romanian cybersecurity laws. The first approach is based on the perspective of regulatory scholars, and the second approach examines the scope of restrictions imposed by the two national laws on the human rights framework. The protection of an individual's human rights can be subject to limitations;

This article was drafted while Lina worked at KU Leuven—The Centre for IT & IP Law.

L. Jasmontaite (✉)
Vrije Universiteit Brussel, Research Group on Law, Science, Technology and Society, Brussels, Belgium
e-mail: lina.jasmontaite@vub.ac.be

V. Pavel Burloiu
Association for Technology and Internet, Bucharest, Romania
e-mail: valentina.pavel@gmail.com

W.J. Schünemann, M.-O. Baumann (eds.), *Privacy, Data Protection and Cybersecurity in Europe*, DOI 10.1007/978-3-319-53634-7_9

however, these limitations must be justifiable, necessary and proportionate. This chapter relies on the legal standard provided by the European Convention on Human Rights (ECHR), European and international human rights instruments as well as the European courts' jurisprudence. Before delving into the analyses of the Lithuanian and Romanian cybersecurity laws and the legislative process employed by both countries, the chapter introduces the underpinning issues related to cyber-security regulation. The contribution reflects on the responsibilities of parties involved in cyberspace regulation, sketches the EU position on the matter and then explains the methodology used to analyse domestic laws and the legislative processes. In the following parts, the Lithuanian and Romanian cybersecurity laws will be introduced. Each description is followed by a section summarising societal reaction and response to new regulatory measures. The authors note that Lithuanian and Romanian societies have different historical backgrounds, however, the authors provide this information only for the purposes of contextual integrity. In each case, the contribution analyses the compatibility of national cybersecurity laws with the human rights framework and the criteria for "good regulation" as described by Robert Baldwin and Martin Cave (see Baldwin and Cave 1999). While reflecting on national perspectives, this chapter underlines the key issues of cybersecurity regulation.

1.1 Who Has a Duty to Protect Cyberspace?

In the debate on cybersecurity, responsibilities of the involved actors are among the most pressing issues on the political agenda on the international (e.g. the United Nations, the Council of Europe), regional (e.g. the EU and the Organization for Security and Co-operation in Europe) and domestic levels. Cybersecurity is a shared concern and responsibility, because compromised cybersecurity (e.g. technical fail-ures, viruses, worms, Trojan horses, etc.) can affect governments, businesses, organisations, and citizens (Wamala 2011). States, individuals, non-governmental organisations and businesses all play an important role with respect to cybersecurity. Some of their roles typically depend on their functions. For example, the financial sector is subject to a stringent regulatory framework, especially when it relates to online services, whereas the role of businesses operating in other fields and that of citizens is rather undefined. However, all actors have a direct impact in cyberspace, irrespective of their roles, actions or lack of action. Therefore, the wide-spread perception that states are among the key duty-bearers for ensuring security in cyberspace does not represent the full reality. Following the rationale of states' positive obligations doctrine, largely developed by the European Court of Human Rights, each state must take measures ensuring the protection of individuals' rights in the digital space, as well as offline. Adopting legislation and setting up infrastruc-ture for the protection of cyberspace (e.g. national Computer Emergency Response Teams and Cyber Security Centres) are among the most popular measures. Further-more, states bear the responsibility for putting in place a workable legal framework and ensuring the collaboration and active participation of all interested parties. Having a legal framework does not intrinsically ensure cybersecurity, since a sound cybersecurity framework is only one of the mechanisms for ensuring a robust security infrastructure.

1.2 Cybersecurity Regulation in the EU

Cyberspace regulation is among the key priorities of the EU. The EU has even developed a cybersecurity strategy despite the disagreement about its competences in this area (European Commission 2013b). The EU cybersecurity strategy paved the way for the adoption of the Network Information Security Directive (NIS Directive), which aims at achieving cyber resilience, reducing cybercrime, developing cyber defence policy and capabilities related to the EU's common security and defence policy, mounting the industrial and technological resources for cybersecurity and establishing a coherent international cyberspace policy for the EU (European Commission 2013a, b).

The EU actions and policy on cybersecurity seem to be primarily driven by economic interests. The EU explains that its cybersecurity strategy aims to prevent losses that European companies experience due to various cybersecurity incidents or breaches. It is roughly estimated that European companies could lose "anything up to US$58 million, with equally significant potential side effects like reputation damage, loss of customers and market share" (European Commission, memo 2013c). Indeed, cybersecurity poses an actual threat for EU-based entities; 93% of large corporations and 76% of small and medium sized enterprises had to address a cybersecurity breach in 2011 (European Commission, memo 2013c).

On the other hand, guaranteeing cybersecurity would contribute to the establishment of a digital single market. The digital single market seeks to ensure free movement of goods, persons, services and capital in the online environment. To establish a well-functioning digital single market "where individuals and businesses can seamlessly access and exercise online activities under conditions of fair competition, and a high level of consumer and personal data protection, irrespective of their nationality or place of residence", one needs to ensure the security of the digital environment (European Commission 2015). It goes without saying that the trustworthiness of the digital environment is a precondition for the EU digital single market to flourish. To this end, the EC has proposed to adopt the NIS Directive.

Before moving to the next section and elaborating on the NIS Directive, it should be noted that the EU ambitions to enhance cyberspace security not seek to only aim at benefiting providers of ICT security products and services, but it also strengthen the EU's role as a human rights actor. The EU is of the position that ensuring security of the digital environment "can have a strong positive impact for the effective protection of fundamental rights, and specifically the right to the protection of personal data and privacy" (Explanatory Memorandum 2013/0027 [COD]).

1.3 Network and Information Security Directive: The Scope and Objectives

The proposal for the NIS Directive was put forward by the European Commission in 2013. The Council of the European Union reached a political agreement with the European Parliament on the core principles of the Directive in December 2015, and the final text of the NIS Directive was adopted in July 2016. It can be anticipated that the NIS Directive will require member states to make adjustments in their legal frameworks governing cybersecurity.

The scope and applicability of the Directive has been a highly debated issue. Initially, the proposed NIS Directive included three categories of providers: online platforms, energy and transport. While this comprehensive approach received support by some countries, it was also perceived as a threat by others as well as by multinational companies. Indeed, under what conditions do cloud computing providers' services fall within the scope of essential services? "Essential services" as proposed by the Council were understood as "services essential for the maintenance of critical societal and economic activities" (Council of the EU, March 2015). At the moment, it seems that each member state will be responsible for identifying

> essential operators to be covered by the directive, based on clear criteria laid down in the text. Particular provisions will be introduced to avoid fragmentation in the identification of operators across member states. However, these are not to undermine member states' prerogatives or security concerns (Council of the EU, 538/2015).

The NIS Directive will serve as an overarching mechanism and provide for a minimum level of security for a digital environment in the EU. It would cover the security of technologies as well as networks. The NIS Directive has the following objectives:

- develop national strategies on cybersecurity (Article 7);
- set up national authorities on the security of network and information systems (Article 8);
- set up national computer incident response teams (CSIRTs) responsible for handling incidents and risks (Article 9) and CSIRTs network (Article 12);
- introduce a cooperation network that would essentially be an enforcement network comprised of national regulators and the European Commission (Article 11);
- introduce an incident notification requirement for companies (Article 14);
- introduce regulatory investigations and audits (Article 15);
- encourage use of relevant security requirements and standards (Article 19); and
- impose sanctions on "infringements of the national provisions adopted pursuant to this Directive" (Article 21).

The NIS Directive constitute a minimum of harmonization measure, which consequently means that it is at the discretion of member states to adopt provisions ensuring a higher level of information system security.

1.4 Measuring Appropriateness of Domestic Cybersecurity Laws

This section lays the groundwork for further analysis measuring the appropriateness of the Lithuanian and Romanian cybersecurity laws. Since appropriateness is a vague concept, it is necessary to consider whether something is right or suited for some purpose or situation. We are inclined to believe that in order to determine the appropriateness of domestic laws, one needs to consider the overall context in which a particular law will function. Is it compatible with the existing regulatory framework, established practices and culture? While the evaluation and interpretation of laws are often subjected to the art of argumentation and rhetoric, it can be based on more substantial criteria found in regulatory theories and jurisprudence.

In the following sections, we follow a five-benchmark test to examine whether the Lithuanian and Romanian cybersecurity laws can be considered good legislation. This test was proposed by Baldwin and Cave in their book titled "Understanding regulation: Theory, strategy and practice". In particular, they suggest evaluating the legislative mandate (e.g. is the discretion of a legislator limited?), the accountability and control mechanisms embedded in the regulatory measure, the process that should entail fair, accessible and open procedures, the level of expertise used to define the regulatory measure, and finally the efficiency of results. When applying the five-benchmark test to both Lithuanian and Romanian cybersecurity laws, we question the extent to which both laws meet the minimum requirements for good regulation. Each section analyses the compatibility of the domestic laws with the fundamental rights framework.

2 Lithuanian Cybersecurity Law

Before the enforcement of the cybersecurity law in January 2015, the Lithuanian regulatory framework governing security in cyberspace was scattered among different sectorial regimes and laws. For example, the Criminal Code of the Republic of Lithuania penalised and sanctions crimes against the security of electronic data and information systems, in other words, criminal acts committed in the digital environment. The Law on Electronic Communication in Article 42 declares unauthorized accessed to information systems or networks illegal. Articles 42[1] and 62 require providers of publicly available electronic communications services or of public communications networks to take technical and organisational measures ensuring security of services and mitigating risks of cyber incidents (LRERĮ 2004).

The Lithuanian cybersecurity law, similarly to the NIS Directive, aims to attribute responsibilities and obligations to actors involved in cybersecurity.

The listed actors include managers and (or) administrators of state information resources, managers of critical information infrastructure, providers of public communications networks, or publicly available electronic communications services and electronic information hosting service providers (ENISA 2013a, b). To ensure the security and reliability of the digital environment, the Lithuanian cybersecurity law provides a framework for risk management, reporting, tackling and prevention of incidents.

According to Article 4 of the Lithuanian cybersecurity law, while the government is responsible for defining the overall objectives and priorities of the national cybersecurity policy, the newly established National Cyber Security Centre, a division of the Ministry of National Defence, is responsible for supervising and coordinating the implementation of the law (Lietuvos Respublikos Kibernetinio Saugumo Įstatymas 2014). Given the highly technical nature of the cybersecurity regulation, Article 9 foresees that the government should receive advice from the Cyber Security Council (Lietuvos Respublikos Kibernetinio Saugumo Įstatymas 2014). Perhaps in order to bring more balance into internet governance on the domestic level, the National Cyber Security Centre will be working closely with the Ministry of Internal Affairs, the Communications Regulatory Authority, the Police Department and the National Data Protection Authority. A collaborative effort is always welcome, but inefficient management of distributed competencies among different public authorities may have a negative impact on the accountability of actions taken by each institution.

The first National Strategy on State Institutions Information Systems and Electronic Information Security was adopted in 2006. The strategy was revised and a more detailed roadmap was presented in the Programme for the Development of Electronic Information Security (Cybersecurity strategy) in 2011. The adoption of a regulatory framework ensuring cybersecurity was among the objectives of the program. Following up on this document, the government proposed the introduction of a law governing cybersecurity in 2013. The adoption of the Lithuanian cybersecurity law followed a special procedure allowing the speeding up of the legislative process. Nonetheless, the legislative proposal was analysed by various institutions and committees. The Committee on Human Rights, the Lithuanian Parliament human rights committee and the National Data Protection Authority found the legislative proposal to be in compliance with the provisions of the European Convention on Human Rights (ECHR) as well as the core principles of data protection.

The Lithuanian cybersecurity law closely resembles the provisions of the proposal for the NIS Directive. Yet the final text of the NIS Directive has been modified through amendments proposed by the European Parliament and the Council. The sections below will not analyse the extent to which the Lithuanian cybersecurity law is aligned with the NIS Directive. Rather, they consider the compatibility of the Lithuanian cybersecurity law with the requirements of "good regulation" and the ECHR.

2.1 What Were the Reactions?

While issues related to cybersecurity score high on the political agenda, it could be stated that they are of little interest to the general public. Only a few concerns about the proposed cybersecurity law were voiced shortly before its adoption by experts and providers of public communications networks, in other words, Internet Service Providers (ISPs). The ISPs raised legitimate concerns about their new obligations with respect to the foreseen cooperation with the law enforcement authorities (Kauno diena 2014). The law professor Mindaugas Kiškis noted that the cybersecurity law entails a paradox: while it aims at fighting external threats to cybersecurity, it will mostly affect Lithuanian citizens and companies (Mano teisės 2015).

In principle, the general public cannot be blamed for being indifferent or unconcerned about the cybersecurity regulation. The fact that only experts expressed their concerns is telling about the lack of transparency and involvement of the broader society. Though the proposal was published on various online portals, the public was neither consulted nor informed about the impact of the proposed regulatory measures. Given that the cybersecurity strategy recognises that cybersecurity concerns "all entities whose activities are related to the provision of services in cyberspace", perhaps it is crucial to find ways to include public institutions, private economic entities, academic society and others in the debate on cybersecurity regulation (Cybersecurity Strategy 2011).

2.2 Controversy of the Lithuanian Cybersecurity Law

The Lithuanian cybersecurity law contains four controversial provisions that require further analysis.

Firstly, per Article 10.3 (6), the National Cyber Security Centre can restrict users' access to the public electronic communication services for 48 h on the basis of a motivated request to the ISP. This measure can be invoked to minimize the impact of a cyber incident on critical information infrastructures and cybersecurity. In situations where orders are needed to restrict access for a longer period, the National Cyber Security Centre is obliged to inform the Communications Regulatory Authority.

Secondly, per Article 12.3, the police can also restrict users' access to the public electronic communication services for 48 h. This can be done only for the purposes of crime investigation and prevention. To restrict access for longer periods than 48 h, the police must obtain a court order.

Thirdly, per Article 12.4, the police can "instruct" providers of public communications networks to allow access to users' metadata. Metadata typically includes the type of service used, time of use, identity of the subscriber, location data, information about accounts and payments made, and other information available to the service provider. The Court of Justice of the EU observed that a combination of different types of metadata "may provide very precise information on the private lives of the persons whose data are retained, such as the habits of everyday life, permanent or temporary places of residence, daily or other movements, activities carried out, social relationships and the social environments frequented" (*Digital Rights Ireland*). Consequently, metadata is considered to be personal or even sensitive data.

To avoid abusive practices, the police department has already adopted an act specifying requirements for such "instructions". According to the implementing act, the instructions must be motivated (well-reasoned) and based on an actual cyber incident that may potentially be regarded as a criminal offence. The underlying objective of such instructions is pre-emptive justice—to investigate available information in order to prevent crime. Provided with these instructions, the request for access to metadata can be carried out via mail or electronic communication means. In particular, the implementing act suggests that this can be done via email, fax or other means. Most importantly, the request must be signed with a qualified electronic signature.

Finally, per Article 16.4, the providers of public communications networks are obligated to provide law enforcement authorities with requested information within eight hours; a shorter period may be provided for in the case of a motivated request submitted by law enforcement authorities.

2.3 New Obligations: What About the Proportionality Principle?

The Lithuanian cybersecurity law provides competent authorities and police with powers to restrict individuals' access to information and unprecedented easy access to individuals' data. In this way, the cybersecurity law may impinge individuals' rights to freedom of expression and privacy. Therefore, the introduction of any limitations on these rights should be subject to a careful balancing exercise.

In general, blocking or restricting access to public communication networks is considered to constitute internet content suppression practices. As such, these practices impede an individuals' possibility to access, receive or impart information and thus impose restrictions on individual's right to freedom of expression as outlined in Article 10 of the European Convention on Human Rights (ECHR). Typically, the law enforcement's actions requesting information about individuals are subject to certain conditions under the EU data protection rules. Only lawful, legitimate and specified laws can interfere with the individual's right to privacy as enshrined in Article 8 of the ECHR. The current situation is worrisome due to the relatively easy access to users' metadata. One can only hope for more proportionate wording once the Lithuanian legislature adapts its current law governing cyberspace to the NIS Directive. In order to be in compliance with human rights, the Lithuanian legislature, as a member of the ECHR club, is required to carry out careful balancing of public and private interests regarding freedom of expression and the right to privacy. Perhaps the legislature will introduce changes in the current legislative framework in the near future. If the legislature remains ignorant to potential threats and limitations imposed on individuals' rights, individual claims can be brought to domestic courts by the affected citizens.

The following section describes the legislative developments concerning the cybersecurity law in Romania. The section will describe two attempts to adopt cybersecurity regulation and the societal reactions to the two legislative endeavours.

3 Romanian Cybersecurity Law

3.1 The First Attempt to Introduce Cybersecurity Regulation

On 30 April 2014, without any public consultation, the Romanian Government sent a draft cybersecurity law to the Romanian Parliament to be voted upon. The proposal envisioned increased data accessing capabilities for the Romanian Intelligence Service (SRI) and nine other public institutions. Access to computer data could have been provided upon a motivated request submitted by a competent authority, without obtaining a court order. The proposed law concerned private legal persons owning, possessing, managing, operating or using an IT system. The text did not indicate what types of data could have been accessed and it did not envision any protection measures in case of data misuse. The proposed law did not require competent authorities, which fall outside the scope of national security exemption, to set personal data protection policies. At the same time, the legislative proposal awarded the SRI a prominent role in information security and failed to provide clear obligations for the subjects of the law.

Without careful consideration of possible implications of the proposed law, after 45 days the Parliament tacitly adopted the proposal, even though the law did not reach the voting agenda of the Chamber of Deputies, as required by the legislative procedure. After this, on 19 December 2014, during the last plenary meeting, the Senate unanimously adopted the law. All that was left for the law to come into force was for the President to sign and promulgate it.

3.2 What Were the Reactions?

The adopted cybersecurity law was strongly criticised by human rights organisations by questioning its adoption process and by voicing major concerns regarding the provisions impinging on individual's rights. Street protests against the law were swiftly organized in several cities across Romania, and several NGOs wrote an open letter to the President asking to stop the law from entering into force. The same letter was sent to Parliament, to the Advocate General as well as to the Supreme Court.

Out of the four entities, only the Supreme Court replied, stating that according to the legal procedures, it did not have enough time to investigate and judge on the matter. The procedure entails summoning all the court's departments, organizing a meeting for deliberation, informing and preparing the judges and writing a response. The legal time for this procedure is usually five days, however, in the cybersecurity case the court had only one day to take care of the complaint.

Following the adoption of the law, Members of Parliament of the Liberal Party raised issues of unconstitutionality and asked the Romanian Constitutional Court to analyse the cybersecurity law. At the same time, 13 non-governmental organisations strongly opposed the formal adoption of the law and supported the unconstitutionality claims expressed by the Members of Parliament by sending an amicus curiae.

On 21 January 2015, the Constitutional Court issued its decision, invalidating the law in its entirety. In its analysis the Court found eight different violations of the Constitution, namely breaches of Articles 1(3) and (5), 21, 23(1), 26, 28, 53, 119, 148 concerning state sovereignty and the rule of law, access to justice, personal freedom and safety, private life, communications secrecy, limitations to the exercise of certain rights or freedoms, respecting the attributions of the Supreme Council for National Defence as well as complying with European Union treaties.

The court's decision followed the reasoning of the Court of Justice of the European Union (CJEU) in decisions such as *Digital Rights Ireland.* It considered prior national jurisprudence which is also echoing CJEU judgement, namely the Constitutional Court's Decision no. 440 of 8 July 2014 on data retention and Decision no. 461 of 16 September 2014 on registering pre-paid SIM card and public Wi-Fi users.

The draft NIS Directive highlighted that cybersecurity attributions must be awarded to civil bodies as sole entities which can democratically offer guarantees for the protection of human rights. In keeping with this principle, the Court also indicated possible coordination issues between the structures at the European level and the military-type structures invested with cybersecurity functions at the national level. In its decision, the Constitutional Court insisted that the need to combat espionage and terrorism cannot be invoked repeatedly to justify any and all cybersecurity measures.

3.3   The Aftermath of the Constitutional Court's Cybersecurity Decision: Data Retention Amendments

After the Court's decision, the President and the political parties met in a series of consultations. Civil society representatives were also invited to informal meetings with the decision makers. Soon after that a new legislation was proposed to modify Law 506/2004 on personal data protection in electronic communications.

Although many points of the new proposal could have been further improved, it includes a number of positive changes. One of the most important new aspects is the requirement for law enforcement authorities to obtain a court order in order to access data. The law also obliges telecommunications operators to delete or anonymize the data collected; this provision is mandatory for data stored for more than three years. The law is only addressing the traffic data, therefore no content data is being stored, collected or shared. Another important aspect is the fact that all retained data must be electronically signed in order to prevent their manipulation and alteration.

Similarly to the first cybersecurity law, the legislative branch again did not consult the public about the new amendments modifying Law 506/2004 on personal data protection in electronic communications. Following up on the positive assessment of the Legislative Committee, the law was adopted in September 2015. This is a spectacular pace for a legislative measure that has not followed the emergency procedure.

In conclusion, it seems that although legislative proposals having an impact on human rights are given slightly greater attention, the pattern of lack of transparency continues. The positive aspect is that civil society in Romania is gradually starting to act as a watchdog. Indeed, society has become more concerned about issues that may impact fundamental rights and freedoms, such as privacy and freedom of speech.

3.4 The Second Attempt to Introduce Cybersecurity Legislation

The Ministry of Communications and Information Society (MCIS) published on 27 January 2016 a new proposal for a cybersecurity law. Several non-governmental organisations immediately demanded more transparency, indicating that the draft law should undergo a public consultation for at least 30 days and insisted that a public debate be organised. The first public consultation meeting was held on 12 February and the second one was organized on 19 February. The Ministry failed to make available the meeting's transcripts and comments submitted by the participants. More than twenty non-governmental organisations and individuals sent an open letter to highlight the numerous inconsistencies and fallacies of the proposals.

It seems that the legislative branch has to a large extent ignored the Constitutional Court's analysis invalidating the first cybersecurity law. The new proposal neither corrects the unconstitutionality aspects, nor does it take into account the text of the NIS Directive. Furthermore, the proposed provisions are not correlated with the national regulatory framework. In addition, Article 4a specifies the underlying principle of the proposed law: to "assure the protection, in cyberspace, of the right to privacy and especially to protect personal data handled by cyber infrastructure holders". In spite of this, the text of the proposal does not even mention Law 677/2001 on the protection of individuals with regard to the processing of personal data. At the same time, the proposal neglects the European recommendations on data breaches and does not take into account the future implementation of the provisions on data breach notifications, as specified in the General Data Protection Regulation.

As mentioned above, the Constitutional Court found eight grounds of unconstitutionality invalidating the first cybersecurity law. The new proposal merely corrected one of them. The previous cybersecurity law allowed different authorities the possibility to access data just by sending a motivated request. The new proposal includes the requirement that access to data has to be granted by a court order. However, as different civil society organisations have pointed out in their comments, Article 20 of the proposal states that cyber infrastructure holders must not allow access to data without the written notification from competent authorities regarding the existence of a court order. Therefore, the provision needs further clarification for excluding the possibility that the authorities will generally invoke court orders for classified national security documents (which cannot be made available to the infrastructure holders). While the court orders for classified national security documents are a valid exception, such clarifications would guarantee that the authorities will not abuse this exception. As to all other aspects, the new proposal does not pass the constitutionality test set by the Constitutional Court.

After undergoing another round of rather superficial public debates, on 4 April 2016, the MCIS published the updated version of the cybersecurity proposal. This intermediary text introduces insubstantial changes, which shows that very few public comments have been incorporated into the updated version. As of the time of writing, there have not been any updates regarding this proposal; therefore, we assume the draft is still in inter-ministerial consultation.

3.5 Impact of Cybersecurity Regulation: Increased Powers of the Intelligence Authority and Legislation on Pre-paid SIM Cards

Recently, the Ministry of Internal Affairs has proposed a new Emergency Government Ordinance to reorganize one of its departments for internal protection as a militarized intelligence unit, granting it national security capabilities with no external control mechanisms and functioning under the command of a military officer appointed by the Ministry. The new service has the potential to become a military unit, performing interceptions without judicial warrant and under no civilian control.

The Brussels attacks in spring 2016 have also produced important after-effects. A new law requiring the mandatory registration of pre-paid SIM cards was announced, and on 6 September 2016, the MCIS published its draft in a less visible section of its website. This is the fifth attempt to introduce this type of law, after the previous three were rejected by the Parliament and the fourth one ruled to be unconstitutional by the Constitutional Court in 2014. Several NGOs heavily criticized the Ministry's proposal and requested to hold a public debate. The law proposal has been suspended.

In conclusion, there have been substantial developments in the cybersecurity sphere with a significant impact on human rights in Romania. A closer look at these developments reveals not only numerous privacy and data protection inconsistencies but also democratic deficiencies and disrespect for the rule of law. In the following section, we will briefly reflect on the way Romanian and Lithuanian cybersecurity laws meet the criteria for a good regulation. This section will also summarise our main findings and suggest topics for further research.

4 Conclusion: Is There a Rule of Thumb?

This article analysed the Lithuanian and Romanian cybersecurity laws. In particular, the article demonstrated how these recently adopted laws contest citizens' fundamental rights and freedoms, such as the right to privacy and freedom of expression. While the analysis of domestic regulatory tools and procedures is at the core of this contribution, the first section presented policy and regulatory developments related to the cybersecurity field in the EU. The authors deem it important to consider the broader context within which domestic measures are supposed to interact and correlate.

Our analysis revealed that while the Lithuanian cybersecurity law somewhat resembles the NIS Directive, the Romanian cybersecurity law seems to be of a broader scope. The latter also appears to be more intrusive in relation to individuals' privacy. At the same time, it can be anticipated that legislative frameworks in both countries will have to be aligned with the provisions of the NIS Directive. Similarly, Lithuania and Romania must report on national laws and other regulatory measures implementing the objectives set by the NIS Directive by 9 May 2018. The likely revision of these laws may affect legal certainty over the applicable rules, as the obligations of the actors involved may be changed repeatedly.

Our analysis of legal provisions and the legislative procedures employed for the adoption of cybersecurity laws challenged the compatibility of the domestic measures with the EU fundamental rights framework as set forth by the EU Charter of Fundamental Rights and the Council of Europe agreements (i.e. the European Convention on the Human Rights and the Convention no. 108). This article sheds light not only on national approaches to cybersecurity regulation but also on a worrisome tendency with respect to internet governance and network stability. Countries are working to develop organisational structures to monitor and minimise threats to cyberspace without sufficiently taking into consideration the rights and interests of the general public and the private sector.

Clearly, there is no rule of thumb for cyberspace regulation and society's reaction to it. While it was observed that Lithuanians have not proactively opposed the cybersecurity law that poses threats to their right to privacy and freedom of expression, Romanian civil society was (partially) successful in voicing its concerns about the proposed legislation. The first legislative proposal to introduce rules on cybersecurity law was declared unconstitutional in Romania.

Furthermore, our analysis showed that national legislative bodies are inclined to trade off the rights of individuals for the purposes of national security. National legislatures remain reluctant to take the extensive jurisprudence developed by the CJEU and European Court of Human Rights (ECtHR) into consideration. Lawmakers should be aware that adopting laws unduly limiting individual rights at the expense of security is not acceptable. As emphasised by the ECtHR, the legal grounds for limiting individual rights contain several requirements. For example, in the case of *AHMET YILDIRIM v. TURKEY* concerning court orders (in third party cases) resulting in the generic blocking of access to online services, the ECtHR, when considering the formal and material criteria for blocking of online service, concluded that a measure "prescribed by law" needs to ensure a certain quality of the regulatory measure. Specifically, the ECtHR ruled that the measure should be precise, accessible to the public, result in predictable outcomes and be compatible with the rule of law.

At the same time, we observed that legal analysis provides answers only to one side of the coin. To have a more thorough understanding of society's reaction to intrusive privacy laws, one should pose many questions. Why did the Lithuanian public accept laws that enhance security at the cost of citizens' privacy? What factors led the Romanian Constitutional Court to invalidate the proposed cybersecurity law even in the aftermath of the Paris and Brussels terrorist attacks? What are the key cultural differences that shape societies' perceptions regarding their rights to privacy and freedom of expression?

Finally, the overall conclusion of our analysis insists on addressing cybersecurity as a complex, inter-dependent ecosystem in which all parties involved—ranging from internet users, academia, and non-governmental organisations to the business sector and governments—share responsibilities. All of these actors should be actively engaged in order to achieve the strongest protection of information communication systems that is compatible with the human rights framework.

References

Baldwin, R., & Cave, M. (1999). *Understanding regulation: Theory, strategy and practice* (pp. 76–85). New York: Oxford University Press.

European Commission. (2013a). *Communication on a digital single market strategy for Europe: An open, safe and secure cyberspace.* Available at https://ec.europa.eu/digital-single-market/en/news/eu-cybersecurity-plan-protect-open-internet-and-online-freedom-and-opportunity-cybersecurity

European Commission. (2013b). *Communication on cybersecurity strategy of the European Union: An open, safe and secure cyberspace.* Available at https://ec.europa.eu/digital-single-market/en/news/eu-cybersecurity-plan-protect-open-internet-and-online-freedom-and-opportu nity-cyber-security

European Commission. (2013c). *Memo on the proposed directive on network and information security – frequently asked questions.* Retrieved April 6, 2016, from http://europa.eu/rapid/press-release_MEMO-13-71_en.htm

European Council. (2015). Press release 538/2015. Retrieved April 6, 2016, from http://www.consilium.europa.eu/en/press/press-releases/2015/06/29-network-information-security/

European Union Agency for Network and Information Security. (2013a). *News from member states: Lithuania – New law on cyber security.* Retrieved April 6, 2016, from https://www.enisa.europa.eu/about-enisa/structure-organization/national-liaison-office/news-from-the-member-states/lithuania-2013-new-law-on-cyber-security

European Union Agency for Network and Information Security. (2013b). *Recommendations on data breach notifications.* Available at https://www.enisa.europa.eu/activities/identity-and-trust/risks-and-data-breaches/dbn

Explanatory Memorandum. (2013). Proposal for a directive of the European Parliament and of the Council concerning measures to ensure a high common level of network and information security across the Union, 2013/0027 (COD).

Government of the Republic of Lithuania. (2011). Resolution No 796 of 29 June 2011 on the Approval of the for the Programme for the Development of Electronic Information Security (Cyber-Security) for 2011–2019. Available at https://www.enisa.europa.eu/topics/national-cyber-security-strategies/ncss-map/Lithuania_Cyber_Security_Strategy.pdf

Kauno diena, Priėmimo išvakarėse Kibernetinio saugumo įstatymo projektas kelia abejonių. (2014). Available at http://kauno.diena.lt/naujienos/lietuva/salies-pulsas/priemimo-isvakarese-kibernetinio-saugumo-istatymo-projektas-kelia-abejoniu-663019

Law no. 506 of 17 November 2004 on the processing of personal data and the protection of privacy in the electronic communications sector. Available in English at http://www.ancom.org.ro/en/uploads/links_files/lege_en_506_2004.pdf

Lietuvos Respublikos Elektroninių Ryšių Įstatymas, 2004 m. balandžio 15 d. Nr. IX-2135, Vilnius, Nr. 69–2382.

Lietuvos Respublikos Kibernetinio Saugumo Įstatymas, 2014 m. gruodžio 11 d. Nr. XII-1428, Vilnius.

Mano teisės. (2015). *Mindaugas Kiškis: Lietuvos kibernetinis saugumas turi būti užtikrintas proporcingomis priemonėmis.* Available at http://manoteises.lt/straipsnis/mindaugas-kiskis-lietuvos-kibernetinis-saugumas-turi-buti-uztikrintas-proporcingomis-priemonemis/

Wamala, F. (2011). (Ph.D.), *ITU National Cybersecurity Strategy Guide, ITU.* Retrieved April 6, 2016, from http://www.itu.int/ITU-D/cyb/cybersecurity/docs/ITUNationalCybersecurityStrategyGuide.pdf

The manufacturer's authorised representative in the EU is Springer
Nature Customer Service Centre GmbH, Europaplatz 3, 69115 Heidelberg,
Germany. If you have any concerns regarding our products, please
contact ProductSafety@springernature.com

Printed and bound by CPI Group (UK) Ltd, Croydon, CR0 4YY
23/04/2026
02095601-0015